THE INTERSECTION

CHANDOS
INFORMATION PROFESSIONAL SERIES
Series Editor: Ruth Rikowski
(email: Rikowskigr@aol.com)

Chandos' new series of books is aimed at the busy information professional. They have been specially commissioned to provide the reader with an authoritative view of current thinking. They are designed to provide easy-to-read and (most importantly) practical coverage of topics that are of interest to librarians and other information professionals. If you would like a full listing of current and forthcoming titles, please visit www.chandospublishing.com.

New authors: we are always pleased to receive ideas for new titles; if you would like to write a book for Chandos, please contact Dr Glyn Jones on g.jones.2@elsevier.com or telephone +44 (0) 1865 843000.

CHANDOS INFORMATION
PROFESSIONAL SERIES

THE INTERSECTION
Where Evidence Based
Nursing and Information
Literacy Meet

Edited by

SUE PHELPS

LOREE HYDE

JULIE PLANCHON WOLF

ELSEVIER

CP
CHANDOS
PUBLISHING
An imprint of Elsevier

Chandos Publishing is an imprint of Elsevier
50 Hampshire Street, 5th Floor, Cambridge, MA 02139, United States
The Boulevard, Langford Lane, Kidlington, OX5 1GB, United Kingdom

Notices

Knowledge and best practice in this field are constantly changing. As new research and experience
broaden our understanding, changes in research methods, professional practices, or medical
treatment may become necessary.

Practitioners and researchers must always rely on their own experience and knowledge in evaluating
and using any information, methods, compounds, or experiments described herein. In using such
information or methods they should be mindful of their own safety and the safety of others, including
parties for whom they have a professional responsibility.

To the fullest extent of the law, neither the Publisher nor the authors, contributors, or editors, assume
any liability for any injury and/or damage to persons or property as a matter of products liability,
negligence or otherwise, or from any use or operation of any methods, products, instructions, or
ideas contained in the material herein.

Library of Congress Cataloging-in-Publication Data
A catalog record for this book is available from the Library of Congress

British Library Cataloguing-in-Publication Data
A catalogue record for this book is available from the British Library

ISBN: 978-0-08-101282-6 (print)
ISBN: 978-0-08-101299-4 (online)

For information on all Chandos publications
visit our website at https://www.elsevier.com/books-and-journals

Working together
to grow libraries in
developing countries

www.elsevier.com • www.bookaid.org

Publisher: Glyn Jones
Acquisition Editor: Glyn Jones
Editorial Project Manager: Thomas Van Der Ploeg
Production Project Manager: Omer Mukthar
Cover Designer: Greg Harris

Typeset by SPi Global, India

Contents

CONTRIBUTORS

Roschelle L. Fritz
Washington State University College of Nursing, Vancouver, WA, United States

Loree Hyde
kpLibraries; Kaiser Permanente, Clackamas, OR, United States

Sue F. Phelps
Washington State University, Vancouver, WA, United States

Kathryn Vela
Washington State University, Spokane, WA, United States

Marian Wilson
Washington State University College of Nursing, Vancouver, WA, United States

AUTHOR BIOGRAPHY

Dr. Marian Wilson is an assistant professor at Washington State University, Spokane. She teaches courses in research and informatics. Her research focuses on engaging nurses in evidence-based practice and improving distressing symptoms using online self-management programs for pain, depression, and sleep. She is certified in pain management nursing from the American Nurses Credentialing Center and American Society for Pain Management Nursing.

Dr. Roschelle L. Fritz is an assistant professor at Washington State University, Vancouver. She teaches courses in research, informatics, and population health and conducts research focusing on the use of health-assistive smart environments for improving patient outcomes. She is a publicly elected hospital commissioner for Washington State Hospital District 1.

Sue F. Phelps is the Health Sciences and Outreach Services librarian at the WSU Vancouver Library. She teaches an online course in Finding Information for Research and provides research assistance for students in the Washington State University College of Nursing. She is passionate about equal access to educational resources for all students and for building a culture of equity on the Vancouver campus.

Loree Hyde is the regional manager of kpLibraries in the Northwest Region. She has a strong focus on evidence-based healthcare and values being part of the clinical decision-making process. She provides mediated searching services for health professionals, as well as information literacy instruction, and serves as a founding member of the Kaiser Permanente NW Evidence-Based Practice and Research Council.

Kathryn Vela is a Health Sciences Outreach librarian at Washington State University, Spokane, and a member of the Academy of Health Information Professionals. She provides reference and information services to the Elson S. Floyd College of Medicine and outreach services to healthcare professionals in rural eastern Washington State.

Julie S. Planchon Wolf is the Research & Instruction/Nursing and Health Studies Librarian at the University of Washington Bothell where she provides online and classroom instruction and assists faculty in designing assignments. She is one of the coauthors of the Information Literacy Competency Standards for Nursing, located online at http://www.ala.org/acrl/standards/nursing.

ACKNOWLEDGMENTS

The editors would like to thank Laura Ziegen, liaison librarian and assistant professor at Oregon Health Sciences University for her contribution to the original document that made this book possible.

Sue Phelps gives enormous thanks to Dr. Karen R. Diller, library director at Washington State University Vancouver, for her support for this project, above and beyond the call of duty.

Loree Hyde would like to thank the faculty of the School of Nursing at the Oregon Health & Science University for their spirit of inquiry and collaboration, especially Debi Eldredge and Diane Bauer.

Julie Planchon Wolf would like to thank her husband Matt Planchon, her mother Dr. Sandra Spiller Wolf, and her supervisor Leslie Hurst, the Head of Teaching & Learning at the University of Washington Bothell and Cascadia College Campus Library, for their support with this project. Thank you to all nurses, nursing librarians, and nursing faculty for the important work you are doing.

Introduction

Sue F. Phelps
Washington State University, Vancouver, WA, United States

This little book came about by way of another project that got completely out of control. In 2011 three members, Julie Planchon Wolf, Loree Hyde, and Sue Phelps, of the Health Sciences Interest Group (HSIG) of the Association of College and Research Libraries (ACRL) began to discuss the possibility of writing an adaptation of the ACRL Information Literacy Competency Standards for Higher Education (ILCSHE) (ACRL, 2000) that focused on nursing. Other disciplines represented in the membership of ACRL had done so, including the Science and Technology Section, from which the HSIG had been conceived. It looked like the task should be fairly straightforward and that health sciences librarians who worked with nurses or nursing students would find the document a useful tool in teaching information literacy for evidence-based practice.

Though there were many combined years of working with nurses and nursing students in the original group of librarians who took on the charge of writing the Information Literacy Competency Standards for Nursing (ILCSN), there was a strong feeling that the values of the nursing profession would be represented with accuracy in the final document. The authors looked to the accrediting bodies for nursing education programs in the, United States, the National League for Nursing Accrediting Commission, Inc. and the Commission on Collegiate Nursing Education, for direction. The two bodies cited a number of documents in their accreditation documents but held in common the American Association of Colleges of Nursing's (AACN) Essentials of Professional Nursing Practice for four segments of nursing education. Though the AACN includes prelicensure nurses in their baccalaureate documnet they did not address the essentials of pre-licensure nursing singly so the librarians looked beyond the Essentials and found a document published by The Quality and Safety Education for Nurses Institute (QSEN) (Cronenwett et al., 2007) directed at education for that population. "Pre-Licensure KSAS" (knowledge, skills, and attitudes) outlined similar concepts to the Essentials documents designed specifically for prelicensure nurses. All documents included the need for skills for graduates consistent with information literacy.

Many other documents were consulted to assure that the Essentials and the KSAS were representative and inclusive as possible, one of which was the RCN Competencies: Finding, using, and managing information: Nursing, midwifery, health, and social care information literacy competencies (RCN, 2011). The Royal College of Nursing identifies information literacy in their professional values and in "the competencies that they intend to support individual and nursing team's thinking about information…" (RCN, 2011, p. 4). The Royal College of Nursing is written for use in the United Kingdom but drew on competencies from Australian and, New Zealand information literacy framework: principles, standards, and practice (2004) which was derived from the ILCSHE (ACRL, 2000). These principles and concepts reach around the globe as evidence-based practice becomes the standard in health care.

Essential Competencies for Evidence-Based Practice in Nursing, 2nd Edition by Kathleen R Stevens was an inspiration for how the authors wished to approach their product. It is a simple table that delineates each competency with the expected skills for each level of education and practice for that competency. It seemed that the same could be written for the nursing essentials and their corresponding ILCSHE. This is where the project got out of control. The resulting document was an unwieldy spreadsheet that did not correspond to the format of any previously published ILCSHE published by ACRL. In fact, it was a document that was found hard to decipher by any of the librarians asked to preview the document. In the end, the ILCSN were written in the established style of the original ILCSHE and the behemoth spreadsheet was set aside.

During that time a couple of things happened. First, ACRL made some changes in the way they approached information literacy. Instead of a collection of the skill outcomes of the information literacy competency standards, they shifted to describing the threshold concepts acquired by those who are gaining literacy in information. This "Framework for Information Literacy for Higher Education" was adopted in 2016 and the original ILCSHE have been rescinded. It is the opinion of the authors of this book that both the ACRL Framework and the ILCSN are compatible documents. They each offer valuable guidance for librarians and nurse educators in the greater concepts of information literacy and in the skills, knowledge, and progression of nursing education to navigate the world of health sciences information. Having learned that a spreadsheet could not convey everything the authors thought was important in their investigation of the nursing documents they were fortunate that, second, Elsevier agreed to publish their findings in the form of a small book. The following is a very brief description of the primary documents used herein.

The Information Literacy Competency Standards for Nursing are based on the original ACRL Information Literacy Competency Standards for Higher Education (ACRL, 2000) which outline specific indicators that identify a student is information literate. It also provides a framework for assessing the information literate individual. It is a set of standards, with performance indicators for each standard and a set of outcomes that specify desired skills. The ILCSN are made specific to nursing through changed language and additional research processes, skills, and resources. They are written to address the progressive expectations for students at the associate, baccalaureate, masters, and doctoral levels and are in support of nursing students, faculty, and librarians in a nursing setting. They can also give administration and curriculum committees a clear understanding of competencies needed by nursing students (ACRL, 2013).

Framework for Information Literacy for Higher Education (FILHE) (2016) is the result of a Delphi study (Townsend et al., 2016) to determine the threshold concepts for information literacy. Threshold concepts "are core ideas and processes in a discipline that students need to grasp in order to progress in their learning, but that are often unspoken or unrecognized by expert practitioners" (Townsend et al., 2016). The Delphi Study (Townsend et al., 2016) identified six threshold concepts central to information literacy which make up the six frames of the FILHE. Each frame, or central concept, is supported by a set of knowledge practices, "ways in which learners can increase their understanding of these information literacy concepts" (ACRL, 2016, p. 2), and dispositions, "which describe ways in which to address the affective, attitudinal, or valuing dimension of learning" (ACRL, 2016, p. 2). The frames are:

- Authority Is Constructed and Contextual
- Information Creation as a Process
- Information Has Value
- Research as Inquiry
- Scholarship as Conversation
- Searching as Strategic Exploration (ACRL, 2016).

The Quality and Safety Education for Nurses Institute (QSEN) (2007) expanded on the Institute of Medicine's competencies for nursing by describing them in relationship to the knowledge, skills, and attitudes that should be developed during pre-licensure nursing education. They cover patient-centered care, teamwork and collaboration, evidence-based practice, quality improvement, safety, and informatics, many of which have a component of information literacy.

The Essentials of Baccalaureate Education for Professional Nursing Practice (2008) set forth the expectations of baccalaureate graduates that will prepare then to work with patients across the lifespan and in the continuum of health care environments. Of the nine essentials outlined by AACN two relate most closely with information literacy. Essential III requires that nursing scholarship be grounded in translating current evidence into nursing practice. Essential IV stresses that information management is critical to the delivery of quality patient care. Baccalaureate education must prepare the nursing student for practice in the 21st century (AACN, 2008).

The Essentials of Master's Education in Nursing (AACN, 2011) are core for all master's programs regardless of focus or future practice setting and build on the baccalaureate nursing practice and guide nurses as they prepare for practice at the doctoral level. The masters level nurse has an advanced level of scientific knowledge and is able to integrate it into practice on an individual or organizational level. Several of the nine Essentials in the masters document have components of information literacy. They speak to scientific findings across diverse settings, ability to articulate quality of methods, measures, and standards, and translate scholarship into practice. In applying research outcomes to practice they not only solve practice problems but also disseminate the results of those changes (AACN, 2011).

The Essentials of Doctoral Education for Advanced Nursing Practice (2006) and The Research-Focused Doctoral Program in Nursing: Pathways to Excellence (AACN, 2010) explain the two main types of doctoral programs in nursing. The Doctor of Nursing Science degree prepares experts in specialized nursing practice while the Doctor of Philosophy degree is research focused. The two types of doctoral programs differ in their goals but both are the highest level of educational preparation in nursing and are rigorous and demanding in their scholarly approach to the profession (AACN, 2006; AACN, 2010).

This book begins with a chapter about evidence-based practice written by Roschelle L. Fritz, PhD, MSN, RN and Marian Wilson, PhD, MPH, RN-BC, who are teaching faculty at Washington State University Vancouver College of Nursing. In that chapter they address what they believe students of nursing science, nursing faculty, and librarians for health sciences need to know about information literacy and evidence based practice. The following six chapters are written by three librarians, Loree Hyde, Sue F. Phelps, and Kathryn Vela, guided by the six frames of the ACRL Framework for

Information Literacy for Higher Education. They each contain how the concepts of the *Framework* and the operational steps of the ILCSN (ACRL, 2013) apply to the essentials of nursing education. The progression of skills and understanding for each level of nursing education is derived from The Quality and Safety Education for Nurses Institute (QSEN) and The American Association of Colleges of Nursing (AACN) Essentials documents. Finally, each chapter is followed by a set of teaching tips. The final chapter offers some thoughts on how information literacy can be integrated into the course work for nursing students and into the routine of practicing nurses.

CONCLUSION

It is the hope of the editors and authors that the content of this out of control project will be useful to the reader in understanding the intersection between nursing and librarianship, providing common understanding of the guiding principles of each discipline and aid in collaborative instruction and scholarship.

REFERENCES

American Association of Colleges of Nursing. (2006). *The essentials of doctoral education for advanced nursing practice.* Retrieved from http://www.aacn.nche.edu/dnp/Essentials.pdf Accessed May 9, 2017.

American Association of Colleges of Nursing. (2008). *The essentials of baccalaureate education for professional nursing practice.* Retrieved from http://www.aacn.nche.edu/education-resources/BaccEssentials08.pdf.

American Association of Colleges of Nursing. (2010). *The research-focused doctoral program in nursing: Pathways to excellence.* Retrieved from http://www.aacn.nche.edu/education-resources/PhDPosition.pdf.

American Association of Colleges of Nursing. (2011). *The essentials of master's education in nursing.* Retrieved from http://www.aacn.nche.edu/education-resources/MastersEssentials11.pdf.

Association of College and Research Libraries. (2000). *Information literacy competency standards for higher education.* Retrieved from http://www.ala.org/acrl/standards/informationliteracycompetency.

Association of College & Research Libraries. (2013). *The information literacy competency standards for nursing.* Retrieved from http://www.ala.org/acrl/standards/nursing.

Association of College & Research Libraries. (2016). *Framework for information literacy for higher education.* Retrieved from http://www.ala.org/acrl/sites/ala.org.acrl/files/content/issues/infolit/Framework_ILHE.pdf.

Cronenwett, L., Sherwood, G., Barnsteiner, J., Disch, J., Johnson, J., Mitchell, P., & Warren, J. (2007). Quality and safety education for nurses. *Nursing Outlook, 55*(3), 122–131.

Royal College of Nursing. (2011). *RCN competencies: Finding, using and managing information: Nursing, midwifery, health and social care information literacy competencies.* Retrieved from https://www2.rcn.org.uk/__data/assets/pdf_file/0005/276449/003053.pdf.

Townsend, L., Hofer, A. R., Hanick, S. L., & Brunetti, K. (2016). Identifying threshold concepts for information literacy: A Delphi study. *Communications in Information Literacy*, *10*(1), 23.

FURTHER READING

Commission on Collegiate Nursing Education. (2009). *Standards for accreditation of baccalaureate and graduate degree nursing programs.* Retrieved from http://www.aacn.nche.edu/ccne-accreditation/standards09.pdf.

International Council of Nurses. (2012). *The ICN code of ethics for nurses*Retrieved from http://www.icn.ch/images/stories/documents/about/icncode_english.pdf.

National League for Nursing Accrediting Commission, Inc. (2008). *NLNAC Accreditation Manual.* Retrieved from http://www.nlnac.org/manuals/Manual2008.htm.

Stevens, K. R. (2005). *Essential competencies for evidence-based practice in nursing.* San Antonio, TX: Academic Center for Evidence-Based Practice.

TIGER Initiative Foundation n.d. *The TIGER initiative: Informatics competencies for every practicing nurse: Recommendations from the TIGER collaborative.* Retrieved from http://www.thetigerinitiative.org/docs/TigerReport_InformaticsCompetencies_000.pdf Accessed 8.28.12.

CHAPTER 1

Evidence-Based Practice in Nursing

Roschelle L. Fritz, Marian Wilson
Washington State University College of Nursing, Vancouver, WA, United States

The use of evidence in the provision of patient care is a national standard of nursing practice in the United States. Nurses practicing in all areas of the discipline (e.g., acute care, clinic, population health) are responsible for providing quality care that optimizes patient outcomes while concurrently conserving resources resulting in cost reduction. Guiding this narrow and sometimes dichotomous path are concepts found within evidence-based practice (EBP) such as use of a systematic and scientific method of inquiry. It is important for nurse educators teaching at all levels (prelicensure, postlicensure, undergraduate, graduate) to teach current and future nurses a systematic process for inquiry. Health sciences librarians play a key role is assisting nurse educators and nurses, both in academia and in clinical practice areas, in using a systematic process of inquiry to discover relevant information and current evidence already available in the literature. Collecting, analyzing, and synthesizing the evidence already in existence is a key to optimizing clinically accurate EBP interventions and identifying new areas of research. Appraising the evidence is foundational to nursing practice and research and to improving the health outcomes of individuals and populations.

1.1 NURSING KNOWLEDGE AND EPISTEMOLOGY

Knowing in the nursing discipline is pluralistic, complex, and multifaceted. It includes concepts from science, theory, practice experience, and disciplinary goals (Chinn & Kramer, 2008; Risjord, 2010). Applied nursing knowledge includes addressing the human's mind, physical body, and their spirit. The quest to understand how to holistically care for ill persons is a never-ending process and having a "spirit of inquiry" is an expected characteristic of all nurses (American Association of Colleges of Nursing, 2008; National League for Nursing, 2017). A baccalaureate prepared nurse should demonstrate an ability to systematically inquire about best practices in caring for a variety of diseases, or for applying up-to-date interventions using evidence-based practice standards. Nurses must also be inquisitive about well-established clinical practices and distinguish between those that remain appropriate and those that may *not* be rooted in science. This is an essential skill for the baccalaureate prepared nurse.

Evidence is one source of the nurse's knowledge. Evidence is that which proves or disproves something or provides grounds for how we care for, or intervene on behalf of, a patient. Historically, this type of knowledge was created through applying the scientific method when solving a problem; however, post-modern evidence encompasses quantitative, qualitative, and mixed methods of discovery. The nursing discipline embraces all three major methodologies and their many associated methods. We additionally value coherence of theory and method.

Nursing is a values-based discipline. Much of nursing knowledge, and therefore our research, infuses concepts of practical worth, beneficence (to health of patient and society) and patients' right to autonomy and self-determination (American Nurses Association, 2011). These values impact the nurses search for new knowledge and may be the premise triggering a search for new information. The goal of providing the best care possible is commonly on the forefront of the nursing mind. Many nurses however, despite their altruistic desires to provide excellent care, admit to not knowing how to seek evidence-based knowledge (Saunders & Vehvilainen-Julkunen, 2015). The literature indicates that over 80% of nurses are familiar with the term evidence-based practice (Cadmus et al., 2008) and greater than 64% express a positive attitude toward evidence-based practice (Majid et al., 2011). Additionally, these nurses believe employing evidence-based practices would improve patient outcomes, yet the majority believe their own knowledge and skills to be insufficient (Saunders & Vehvilainen-Julkunen, 2015). Furthermore, nurses admit that the library is not where they go to get information (Cadmus et al., 2008). Rather, they most commonly report using trusted peers and colleagues as the primary source (Pravikoff, Tanner, & Pierce, 2005). This may result in nurses not using evidence in their practice, or not practicing in ways that align with current scientific evidence. For example, nurses may be taught informally by colleagues that a particular method of infection control is unnecessary, such as disinfecting stethoscopes between each patient use. Therefore, they may routinely avoid the extra step of disinfecting equipment between patients. Such beliefs could result in an increased risk to patients of preventable nosocomial infections. Alternatively, when nurses learn the burden of contamination present on stethoscopes through scientific evidence, they may be more likely to practice in ways that protect patients from harm. Nurses are faced with numerous daily practice decisions that allow them to choose whether to behave in alignment with scientific evidence, or to rely on workplace norms. These revelations should be a wake-up call to nurse educators and librarians of the importance of guiding and training nurses on how to obtain topic appropriate evidence worthy of application in practice. It is within the role of the librarian to assist nurses in finding and comprehending the evidence that can most effectively guide their practice. As a result, the librarian can influence patient care outcomes every bit as much as the nurse.

There is also a wide spectrum of education and experience levels among nurses. The entry level to practice is an associate degree, which includes an introduction to evidence-based practice (commonly infused throughout several courses) and an emphasis on utilization of best practices. At the Associate Degree level the primary focus is training the student to perform skills such as starting an intravenous line or placing a nasogastric tube and assessing and reporting on the patient. Another main focus is developing critical thinking skills. For the associate-prepared nurse, best practice knowledge and information are primarily sought from policy and procedure manuals, which are supported with evidence-based citations. In contrast, the baccalaureate-prepared nurse will take at least one course specifically focusing on research and evidence-based practice. However, skill levels may vary, whereby some baccalaureate nurses will feel very comfortable seeking and reading professional journal articles to address their scientific questions, while others may feel this is a task best left to administrators and quality improvement experts. The Master's level and beyond is where most nurses (not all) finally become truly familiar with seeking evidence and applying it to practice because they, generally, will have to show mastery to earn their degree. Yet, with the recent advent of many online graduate programs, range of skills and abilities can vary dramatically. Librarians and nurse educators should not assume all Master's-prepared nurses are well prepared to access and appraise research evidence just because they have an advanced degree. It may be prudent to evaluate each individual's skill and comfort with research resources when assisting with a search for evidence.

It is important to note that the majority of nurses practicing at the bedside (on the frontline) have an associate or baccalaureate degree. The lack of graduate level prepared nurses may be one reason the nursing discipline struggles with a practice-theory gap.

Additionally, 44% of nurses are age 50 or over (National Council of State Boards of Nursing, 2015). These more senior nurses may perceive that concepts of EBP are for the younger nursing generation and they may not have been taught, or even believe, these concepts (Wilson et al., 2015); despite EBP being an expected nursing role. Nurses from organizations that support EBP and who take advantage of clinical ladder and research opportunities, as well as advancing skills through certifications and advanced degrees, are more likely to feel prepared to engage in EBP (Wilson et al., 2015).

1.2 EVIDENCE-BASED PRACTICE MODELS

In this section, we discuss the value of using evidence-based practice models and highlight three models commonly used in clinical practice. We describe nurses' application of these models in clinical practice and discuss several barriers to implementation.

Evidence-based practice models are valuable because they help the nurse ask a clinical question, so a clinically based answer might be discovered. Many EBP nursing courses teach models to assist nurses in navigating commonly presented steps of EBP: ask the research question, access the evidence, appraise the evidence, and apply the evidence. We find that Registered Nurse students transitioning from an associate degree to a baccalaureate degree (RN-BSN) typically do not have experience with any of the foundational steps of EBP. Therefore, we begin with the most basic element of asking a focused clinical question. We instruct these nurses regarding:

(a) Where current evidence comes from?

(b) How to effectively search and organize information?

(c) How to critically appraise and synthesize the evidence?

Using a model, such as the ones described later, facilitates an organized and consistent approach for discovering and providing evidence-based nursing care solutions.

Nursing is a practice-based discipline. Nurses seek evidence that can be applied in clinical practice; meaning, evidence that will guide decisions and the hands-on interventions performed on fellow human beings. The stakes are often high and using evidence-based interventions provides nurses with increased assurance that they are optimizing care and improving outcomes. However, application of evidence in nursing cannot be a "one-size-fits-all" activity because nursing is a diverse and varied discipline. Features that require consideration for librarians assisting in a search for evidence may include:

(a) The area of nursing practice?

(b) Frontline care versus support to frontline nursing practice (e.g., bedside versus administration or quality improvement)?

(c) Research methods used as it regards the question?

(d) Availability of information (i.e., whether or not information exists on the topic of interest)?

(e) Nurse's ability to discern quality and strength of available evidence? Each feature provides a lens which can frame a search.

Three models are commonly used to assist incorporating evidence into clinical practice: Advancing Research and Clinical Practice through Close Collaboration (ARCC), the Iowa Model, and the Johns Hopkins Model. See Table 1.1 for a description of the differences and similarities. All three are good models with many common attributes; however, nurses should

Table 1.1 Differences and similarities in evidence-based practice models

Model	Components	Unique attributes
Advancing Research and Clinical Practice through Close Collaboration© (ARCC)	Cultivate a spirit of inquiry and culture of research Identify a PICOT question Collect relevant evidence Critically appraise evidence using pyramid Make practice decision, change practice Evaluate outcomes of practice change Disseminate findings	Infuses Cognitive Behavioral Theory for promoting EBP change within a healthcare system Readiness and implementation evaluation scales Using PICOT for focused clinical question development Emphasis on EBP mentors to assist in thinking and feeling about EBP implementation Use of a pyramid for appraising the evidence
Iowa	Problem identification Assessing organizational priorities is stressed Forming a team Critique of relevant literature Implementing practice change Dissemination of findings	Differentiates between problem-focused triggers and knowledge-focused triggers Recommends piloting the change before large-scale implementation Allows for practice change based on evidence that includes expert opinion and theory
Johns Hopkins	Practice question Evidence Translation	PET: easy to remember acronym Tools (worksheets) available to step nurse through the process Nonresearch evidence can systematically be included (e.g., informatics data, patient preference)

look to their clinical setting to align with a model that has been selected by their nursing leaders. If no model has been designated, nurses can be encouraged to select one that best suits their particular environment. Nurses can also influence their organizations by advocating for an agreed-upon model that will facilitate success in implementing EBP. Medical librarians can play a role in healthcare organizations by introducing EBP models and teaching how they can facilitate consistent delivery of evidence-based care. It is also helpful if librarians have a working knowledge of EBP models, so they can guide nurses through the steps because the nurse may be unfamiliar with such processes.

1.2.1 Advancing Research and Clinical Practice Through Close Collaboration

In this model, emphasis is placed on organizational culture and having a spirit of inquiry that can result in adoption of changes (Melnyk & Fineout-Overholt, 2015; Schaffer, Sandau, & Diedrick, 2013). Nurses are encouraged to follow a template using the acronym PICOT (Population, Intervention, Comparison, Outcome, Time) to guide development of a clinically relevant and searchable question. The question should regard a specific population, identify an intervention (e.g., increasing amount of time between emptying urine catheter bag), identify a comparison (i.e., to a current standard of care), seek a specified outcome, and be time oriented. Thereafter, a search is conducted across databases, and evidence is collected, appraised, and synthesized using a pyramid whereby the base contains lesser quality evidence and the top contains highest quality evidence. For more information on ARCC we recommend Melnyk and Fineout-Overholt's book, *Evidence-Based Practice in Nursing and Healthcare: A Guide to Best Practice* (See Melnyk & Fineout-Overholt, 2015).

1.2.2 Iowa Model

This model is comprised of a multistep process, whereby nurses can focus on problem- or knowledge-based practice issues. The identified issue becomes the initiator of practice change. The Iowa Model begins with identifying the problem or knowledge gap, and then the organization decides if addressing the issue is a priority. Evidence is then gathered and analyzed. Proposed practice changes are piloted on a small scale and if there is sufficient quality evidence, changes are made on a larger scale. Following the implementation steps, an evaluation of care quality and patient outcomes is completed. For more information on the Iowa Model, we recommend Titler et al. (2001).

1.2.3 John's Hopkins Model

This model includes resource tools to assist the nurse in searching for evidence. Though this model can be summed up in three steps (Practice Question, Evidence, Translation), each step contains several important detailed components. Factors impacting practice are categorized as internal versus external. Internal factors are culture, environment, equipment/supplies, staffing, and standards. External factors are accreditation, legislation, quality measures, regulations, and standards. Both internal and external factors additionally affect research and education. Ways of knowing are separated into "research" and "nonresearch." "Research" includes studies that are ranked by impact. They are, from highest impact to lowest: experimental, quasiexperimental, nonexperimental, qualitative. "Nonresearch" includes information from sources such as an organization's quality or financial data, clinical expertise, and patient preference. For resource tools, see Johns Hopkins Medicine (2017).

1.3 BARRIERS TO IMPLEMENTATION

Although the Institute of Medicine's (IOM) goal is that 90% of clinical decisions be evidence-based by 2020 (IOM, 2009) knowledge regarding EBP varies greatly among frontline nurses. However, learning about EBP may empower nurses with a spirit of inquiry and the courage to suggest and/or implement practice changes. Nurses employed at hospitals committed to nursing excellence, such as those seeking Magnet® designation, and educated at the baccalaureate level or higher, demonstrate higher EBP ability, desire, and frequency of behaviors (Wilson et al., 2015). Nevertheless, many nurses indicate that they encounter multiple barriers to implementation of EBP.

Most barriers are common across multiple practice areas, though there may be specific barriers by area of practice (e.g., perioperative). Barriers can be generally categorized as institutional or personal. See Table 1.2 for a summary of barriers identified in the extant literature. Institutional barriers are those that regard organizational culture, administrative resources, and staffing or budgetary constraints. Institutional barriers may be the hardest to address due to broadness of ownership; meaning, no single person can make a sweeping change and collaboration by multiple people in multiple departments is necessary. Nurses cite institutional barriers as lack of time and resources and lack of administrative support, even administrative opposition, as reasons for not engaging in EBP (Cadmus et al., 2008; Koehn & Lehman, 2008; Majid et al., 2011; Melnyk, Fineout-Overholt, Gallagher-Ford, & Kaplan, 2012; Ross, 2010; Shifaza, Evans, & Bradley, 2014).

Table 1.2 Barriers to evidence-based practice implementation

Institutional	Personal	Situational
Lack of time	Lack of general knowledge of EBP	Lack of high-quality research on the topic of interest
Lack of administrative support	Lack of skills to critique and analyze research	Stakeholders not convinced value of attention to the topic at hand
Resistance from managers and leaders	Lack of research vocabulary	Emergent regional healthcare issues arise absorbing any extra resources (e.g., pandemic)
Lack of financial resources	Lack of understanding of statistical terms	Nurses historically not seen as integral to research process
Little or no access to databases	Lack of search skills	Inconsistent presentation of research and EBP in nursing school curricula
Organizational culture: Insufficient spirit of inquiry	Lack of understanding of database characteristics	Relevant literature not compiled in one place
Absence of EBP mentors at point of care	Lack of desire for EBP	

Personal barriers mostly involve a lack of knowledge, which education can remedy. Nurses report a knowledge deficit regarding:

(a) Organization and structure of databases

(b) Retrieving relevant research articles

(c) Reading and understanding the language used in research articles

(d) Statistical terms

(e) Synthesizing the literature

One personal barrier that may or may not be remedied by education is attitude. Depending on previous positive or negative clinical EBP experiences, nurses' attitudes on EBP will vary. Nurses exposed to EBP under stressful circumstances (e.g., lack of support, unrealistic expectations) may initially resist learning about EBP. Nurses have been found less likely to perceive themselves as ready to engage in EBP if they have bedside clinical roles and report difficulty understanding the research process and research articles (Wilson et al., 2015). Patience will be needed on the part of librarians and nursing faculty. Creative and "out-of-the-box" approaches to engagement may help these students. Finding opportunities to engage nurses in research projects may be the single most important way to increase nurses' confidence and readiness for EBP (Wilson et al., 2015). Once nurses can see the relevance of EBP to their daily practice, their attitudes are more favorable. Also, as students experience increased self-efficacy and ability with EBP skills, they report a greater desire to engage in EBP activities (Wilson, Bryant, Schenk, & Amiri, 2016).

Other barriers identified by nurses are a lack of access to databases (Cadmus et al., 2008; Pravikoff et al., 2005; Ross, 2010), relevant material is not compiled in one place (Shifaza et al., 2014), and lack of search skills (Cadmus et al., 2008; Koehn & Lehman, 2008; Pravikoff et al., 2005; Saunders & Vehvilainen-Julkunen, 2015; Wilson et al., 2015). Nurses tend to use basic search features and most are not familiar with Boolean and proximity operators.

One additional barrier has emerged over the last 2 decades, the closing of hospital-based libraries. Hospital-based libraries and medical librarians are a scarce resource in modern healthcare. Many students and practicing nurses, even those working within large tertiary healthcare systems, no longer enjoy the benefit of meeting with a medical librarian and searching library texts onsite or online. Hospitals rarely subscribe to major medical databases, adding to the difficulty of accessing information. In response to this concern, the State Board of Nursing in some states now collaborate with state universities to provide limited access to online databases, such as Washington State's HEALWA program.

1.4 SOURCES OF EVIDENCE

In this section, we discuss four important emerging scientific fields with high impact and clinical relevance. We also highlight electronic health record (EHR) informatics reporting as a separate but clinically utilized source of evidence. It is important for librarians and nurse educators to become familiar these fields because some of the most relevant information to support nursing practices maybe found within them.

The four emerging sciences are prevention science, practice and translational science, epigenetics and genomics, and multidisciplinary research. Knowledge from these fields is impacting nursing knowledge. Concepts from these fields are becoming foundational to some evidence-based guidelines.

Prevention Science. Literature from the field of prevention science is informing the approach to treatment of chronic conditions such as heart disease, diabetes, kidney disease, stroke, and other neurological disorders. Prevention science literature provides information pertinent to nurses performing patient education. A major component of all patient education regards how to prevent repeated exacerbation scenarios, which includes content regarding lifestyle changes for improved health and recovery. The importance of assisting patients in their road to recovery while concurrently educating on how to prevent future events is now more important than ever. Changes in reimbursement from the Center for Medicare Services (CMS) for the care of older adults, along with the implementation of the Affordable Care Act, has resulted in an overall move in the United States' healthcare system from a fee-for-service payment model to value-based care. The reality for many hospitals and providers is that patient outcomes must improve, and they must demonstrate that improved outcomes are sustainable. CMS is asking that evidence be provided through quality measure reporting; otherwise reimbursement will be reduced or withdrawn.

An example scenario is a patient with congestive heart failure who is seen in the emergency department (ED) and released but returns to the ED within 30 days for additional treatment of the same condition. If the patient returns too soon, the visit will be categorized as a readmission and the hospital will not be reimbursed for any care provided during that second visit, including an acute hospitalization. The hospital itself will be financially responsible for the additional care. CMS enforces this through a new payment system called "bundled payments." Bundled payments are also known as episode payments and are a designated rate for all care related to a single exacerbation episode. The financial impact of bundled payments has resulted in employers (e.g., hospital systems, providers) placing high priority on patient education, so patient reentry into the system may be avoided. Prevention science literature contains EBP data that nurses can use for providing this education. It also provides persuasive data on chronic disease symptom-reversing lifestyle changes and data that allows populations to remain well. Additionally, it includes literature on motivational interviewing, an effective technique employed by nurses during patient education sessions that can assist patients in initiating behavioral changes to improve health outcomes.

Practice and Translational Science. Translational research is important to nursing because it addresses the ever-looming theory-practice gap. Translational scientists seek to understand the impact of interventions. Because nurses are in essence interventionists, this body of literature directly informs nursing practice by providing evidences-based ideas regarding implementation of EBP research. Best practice guidelines are, at times, difficult to implement in a practical way. For example, an acute care nurse recently piloted an EBP project on oral care for nonventilated hospital-acquired pneumonia (NV-HAP) patients at a hospital in Washington State (Berry, 2017). The literature indicated oral care should likely be provided every 6 hours to match the rate of replication of microorganisms, yet this would not be practical to ask of nurses. The result of this practice project was a recommendation to implement oral care twice daily for reducing NV-HAP. Results provided evidence for a practical recommendation that likely *translates* to decreased NV-HAP. Translational science literature offers frontline nurses reasonable EBP implementation ideas that can realistically be used in fast-paced high-stakes environments.

Epigenetics and Genomics. Studies that regard the impact of heritage and social determinates of health are of particular importance to nursing. Nursing is a field that lies at the boundary of social science and biomedical science. Research that combines social and biological health concepts are well positioned to have clinical relevance. Nurses working in community and population health, environmental nursing, and case management would be particularly interested in this area, though research findings in these areas are applicable across all nursing. The road to value-based care will include knowledge and infusion of ideas from epigenetics and genomics. Nurses who understand the concepts of genomics can influence medication decisions. For example, certain genetic variations can contribute to individual differences in an antidepressants' response (GENDEP Investigators, MARS Investigators, & STAR★D Investigators, 2013).

Multidisciplinary Research. Nurses practicing in the clinical setting are already familiar with a multidisciplinary approach to care. However, these same nurses may need guidance regarding how to search for and select articles that specifically provide multidisciplinary solutions to practice-based challenges. Multidisciplinary solutions are a modern-day expectation in the clinical practice setting. Solutions to clinical problems can be found within many sources of information beyond strictly "nursing" journals. Librarians can assist nurses in searching diverse databases that store studies from pertinent disciplines, such as psychology, anthropology, physical therapy, medicine, or engineering.

1.5 INFORMATICS AS EVIDENCE

The Health Information Technology for Economic and Clinical Health (HITECH) Act was enacted as part of the American Recovery and Reinvestment Act of 2009. The HITECH Act called for widespread implementation of EHRs. It promoted the meaningful use of EHRs by tying reimbursement to patient outcomes, which were measured and reported as quality indicators. This patient outcome quality data can be retrieved through the EHRs reporting functions. Outcomes from early reporting across EHRs led to the emergence of new concepts in healthcare. They are: care transitions, dashboards for quality measures, computerized physician order entry (CPOE), eligible professionals (EP), evidence-based clinical decision support (CDS), and health information technology (HIT). See Table 1.3 for a brief description of each. Knowledge of these concepts and common language used around them will provide contextual breadth when searching in a wide variety of clinical topic areas.

The electronic health record (EHR) is a powerful tool providing patient and population health data. All major EHRs have the capability of reporting on a wide variety of patient outcomes and quality care indicators. These are often referred to as informatics reports. Clinical decisions are made, and care programs are implemented, based on data retrieved from these reports. Often, unit policies and/or practice guidelines will shift based on these reports. Therefore, nurses perceive informatics reports as a form of evidence

Table 1.3 Meaningful use concepts

Care transitions	The point in care where the patient moves along the continuum of care, often involving a change in physical location (e.g., acute care hospital to rehabilitation skilled nursing center) and a change in caregivers and/or providers. Movement is bidirectional.
Quality measures	Indicators that are specifically defined and which represent diminished, improved, or status quo patient outcomes. Measures may be department, unit, and population specific.
Dashboards	A graphic representation of compiled data that highlights an organizations performance. It allows easy visualization of critical performance issues. Used by organizations to simplify quality reporting and analysis.
CPOE	Computerized physician order entry (CPOE) of treatment regimens and medications.
EP	"Eligible professionals" or hospitals successfully attest to or demonstrate meaningful use of EHRs.
CDS	"Clinical decision support" is offered in EHRs via intelligent algorithms, which guide availability of choices for data entry in the EHR.
HIT	Health information technology. Technologies used in a learning healthcare system (e.g., EHR, cloud-based computing).

upon which to base their practice. For example, if a report provides evidence that a particular unit has more patient falls than other hospital units, a fall prevention program may need to be implemented. Here, the clinical nurse and/or manager may search for EBP literature for ideas on programs and evidence of what techniques result in the greatest reduction of falls. In this way, the informatics report leads to the search for EBP literature. Ultimately, both sets of information (informatics report and EBP patient fall literature) are perceived as evidence used to support a practice change.

1.5.1 Future Evidence

Big data is derived from continuous monitoring technologies and is positioned to be a future source of informatics evidence. Smart environments and the data from Internet of Things (I.O.T) are a by-product of the connectedness of the modern world. Technologies used in these smart and connected environments produce large amounts of data. Data analytics is emerging as an important part of health science because of the number of data points that can be measured with regard to health outcomes. Some data points can be derived from EHRs, while other data points are derived from implanted, wearable, and ambient sensors used by patients (e.g., implanted medication pump, smart watch, health-assistive smart home). Data-driven health may also be part of the transition from fee-for-service to value-based models of care.

1.6 HEALTH POLICY AND EVIDENCE-BASED PRACTICE

Major policies and laws driving healthcare in the United States include provisions for EBP. The Institute for Healthcare Improvement's Triple Aim (Institute for Healthcare Improvement, 2017) focuses on three dimensions of performance in healthcare for the purpose of optimizing patient outcomes and national health. These are improving the patient experience (quality and satisfaction), improving the health of populations, and reducing per capita costs. Evidence-based practice is the driving force connecting the dimensions of improved quality and cost reduction. The Center for Medicare Services (CMS) identifies specific quality measures that hospitals and providers must report on to receive maximum reimbursement for provided care. Currently enough data to drive goal setting exists, and improvements are expected over time. Improvements will be associated with reimbursement rates. CMS reporting requirements and the potential loss of revenue have prompted hospitals to change practices and to align with Triple Aim goals. Research around optimal care provisions for sustainable outcomes gained a lot of attention in the clinical setting because this evidence can be used to guide organizations toward better outcomes at lower cost.

Several other reports and standards are impacting the EBP movement in the clinical setting. The Institute of Medicine's (IOM) *Healthy People 2020* (Department of Health and Human Services, 2010) report highlights the importance of addressing specific segments of the population and can be used as a guide when deciding which research areas are highest priority and what questions need answered first. The IOM's 2011 report *The Future of Nursing: Leading Change, Advancing Health* is an excellent guide for nurses wanting to promote EBPs. This IOM report indicates that nurses need higher levels of education and training and that workforce planning and policy require better data collection and information infrastructures. The Quality and Safety Education for Nurses (QSEN) Institute (2014), which guides curriculum development through setting competency standards, highlights the importance of quality, safety, and information and calls for nurses to utilize EBP to optimize care. Additionally, the HITECH Act of 2009 (HealthIT.gov, 2016) calls for information technology to be used in a meaningful way, to support Triple Aim dimensions. Finally, the American Nurses Association's (2011) *Code of Ethics* and *Standards of Practice* addresses factors effecting patient care, including declarations that EBP is an expected nursing role and nurses should be involved in creating evidence.

1.7 ROLE OF EVIDENCE IN FUTURE OF NURSING PRACTICE

The IOM released a summary in 2015 on the United States' healthcare system, which included the term a "learning healthcare system." The IOM defined healthcare as a system in which "science, informatics, incentives, and culture are aligned for continuous improvement and innovation, with best practices seamlessly embedded in the delivery process and new knowledge captured as an integral by-product of the delivery experience" (IOM, 2015). In this "learning system" evidence is the basis for implementing change. As evidence is created and analyzed, and changes are implemented and evaluated, findings are fed back into the system, so "learned" information can be used to support further change. Evidence-based practice is a key piece of this system, which is represented as a circular feedback loop of input and output (Fig. 1.1).

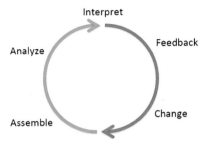

Fig. 1.1 The learning healthcare system cycle. (Reprinted with permission.) Process by which all healthcare systems functionally continue to improve, optimizing patient outcomes. System has three components: Afferent (*blue*, on left) assemble and analyze data, Efferent (*red*, on right) feed findings back into practice and make changes, and Scale (can be institutional, national, international).

Future nurses and librarians supporting nurses in their quest for evidence will benefit from understanding the role of EBP in a learning healthcare system. For more information on the Learning Healthcare System, see IOM (2011) and The Learning Healthcare Project (2017).

1.8 CONCLUSION

In this chapter, we addressed how nurses know what they know and how they integrate EBP in the clinical setting. We provided a framework for conceptualizing EBP solutions within a complex learning healthcare system where clinical practice is impacted by changing healthcare laws and financial structures. We discussed barriers to implementing EBP and highlighted EBP models commonly used in the clinical setting. We discussed the important role the fields of prevention, translational, epigenetics and genomics, and multidisciplinary sciences are playing with regard to EBP in nursing. We also proposed that EHRs and informatics reports are considered a form of evidence that informs practice and hinted that Big Data and data analytics will be a major source of future evidence that is relevant to practice. Librarians and nurse educators reading this chapter should recognize that nursing knowledge is pluralistic and multifaceted, that scientific evidence is a valued way of knowing, but that many nurses are not well versed in systematically approaching and appraising the evidence. Librarians understanding the unique needs of nurses can assist in providing tailored information support. Ultimately, this can create a critical partnership among librarians and nurse educators as they join nurses in the delivery of evidence-based healthcare.

REFERENCES

American Association of Colleges of Nursing. (2008). *Leading initiatives: Essentials series.* Retrieved from http://www.aacn.nche.edu/education-resources/essential-series. Accessed 04.04.17.

American Nurses Association. (2011). *Nursing code of ethics.* Retrieved from http://www. nursingworld.org/Mobile/Code-of-Ethics. Accessed 04.01.17.

Berry, S. (2017). The role of oral care in the prevention of hospital acquired pneumonia in non-ventilated patients. In Western Institute of Nursing Research Conference, Denver, CO.

Cadmus, E., Van Wynen, E. A., Chamberlain, B., Steingall, P., Kilgallen, M. E., Holly, C., et al. (2008). Nurses' skill level and access to evidence-based practice. *Journal of Nursing Administration, 38*(11), 494–503.

Chinn, P. L., & Kramer, M. K. (2008). *Integrated theory and knowledge development in nursing* (7th ed.). St. Louis, MO: Mosby.

Department of Health and Human Services. (2010). *Healthy people 2020.* Retrieved from http://www.healthypeople.gov/2020/about/DisparitiesAbout.aspx. Accessed 03.16.17.

GENDEP Investigators, MARS Investigators, STAR★D Investigators. (2013). Common genetic variation and antidepressant efficacy in major depressive disorder: A meta-analysis of three genome-wide pharmacogenetic studies. *The American Journal of Psychiatry, 170*(2), 207–217. https://doi.org/10.1176/appi.ajp.2012.12020237.

HealthIT.gov. (2016). *Health IT legislation and regulations.* Retrieved from https://www. healthit.gov/policy-researchers-implementers/health-it-legislation. Accessed 05.21.17.

Institute for Health Improvement. (2017). *Initiatives: IHI triple aim initiative.* Retrieved from http://www.ihi.org/Engage/Initiatives/TripleAim/Pages/default.aspx. Accessed 05.21.17.

Institute of Medicine. (2011). Report of the Committee on the Robert Wood Johnson Foundation Initiative on the Future of Nursing. In *The future of nursing: Leading change, advancing health.* Washington, D.C.: National Academies Press.

Institute of Medicine. (2015). Leadership consortium for value & science-driven health care. In *The learning health system series: Continuous improvement and innovation in health and health care.* Washington, D.C.: National Academies Press. (Accessed 09.08.17).

Institute of Medicine (US) Roundtable on Evidence-Based Medicine. (2009). *Leadership commitments to improve value in healthcare: Finding common ground: Workshop summary.* Washington (DC): National Academies Press (US). Available from: https://www.ncbi. nlm.nih.gov/books/NBK52847/.

Koehn, M. L., & Lehman, K. (2008). Nurses' perceptions of evidence-based nursing practice. *Journal of Advanced Nursing, 62*(2), 209–215. https://doi.org/10.1111/j.1365-2648.2007.04589.x.

Majid, S., Foo, S., Luyt, B., Zhang, X., Theng, Y., Chang, Y., & Mokhtar, I. (2011). Adopting evidence-based practice in clinical decision making: Nurses' perceptions, knowledge, and barriers. *Journal of the Medical Library Association, 99*(3), 229–236.

Melnyk, B., & Fineout-Overholt, E. (2015). *Evidence-base practice in nursing and healthcare: A guide to best practice* (3rd ed.). Philadelphia: Wolters Kluwer Health.

Melnyk, B. M., Fineout-Overholt, E., Gallagher-Ford, L., & Kaplan, L. (2012). The state of evidence-based practice in US nurses. *JONA: The Journal of Nursing Administration, 42*(9), 410–417. https://doi.org/10.1097/NNA.0b013e3182664e0a.

National Council of State Boards of Nursing. (2015). *National nursing workforce study.* Retrieved from https://www.ncsbn.org/workforce.htm. Accessed 05.21.17.

National League for Nursing. (2017). *NLN competencies for graduates of nursing programs.* Retrieved from http://www.nln.org/professional-development-programs/competencies-for-nursing-education/nln-competencies-for-graduates-of-nursing-programs. Accessed 04.25.17.

Pravikoff, D. S., Tanner, A. B., & Pierce, S. T. (2005). Readiness of U.S. nurses for evidence-based practice. *American Journal of Nursing, 105*(9), 40–51.

QSEN Institute. (2014). *Competencies.* Retrieved from http://qsen.org/competencies/. Accessed 05.21.17.

Risjord, M. (2010). *Nursing knowledge: Science, practice, and philosophy.* New Delhi, India: Wiley-Blackwell.

Ross, J. (2010). Information literacy for evidence-based practice in perianesthesia nurses: Readiness for evidence-based practice. *Journal of Perianesthesia Nursing, 25*(2), 64–70. https://doi.org/10.1016/j.jopan.2010.01.007.

Saunders, H., & Vehvilainen-Julkunen, K. (2015). The state of readiness for evidence-based practice among nurses: An integrative review. *International Journal of Nursing Studies,* https://doi.org/10.1016/j.ijnurstu.2015.10.018.

Schaffer, M. A., Sandau, K. E., & Diedrick, L. (2013). Evidence-based practice models for organizational change: Overview and practical applications. *Journal of Advanced Nursing, 69*(5), 1197–1209. https://doi.org/10.1111/j.1365-2648.2012.06122.x.

Shifaza, F., Evans, D., & Bradley, H. (2014). Nurses' perceptions of barriers and facilitators to implement EBP in the Maldives. *Advances in Nursing, 2014,* 1–7. https://doi.org/10.1155/2014/698604.

The Learning Healthcare Project. (2017). *Background: The learning healthcare system.* Retrieved from http://www.learninghealthcareproject.org/section/background/learning-healthcare-system%0D. Accessed 05.19.17.

Titler, M. G., Kleiber, C., Steelman, V. J., Rakel, B. A., Budreau, G., Everett, C., et al. (2001). The Iowa model of evidence-based practice to promote quality care. *Critical Care Nursing Clinics of North America, 13*(4), 497–509.

Wilson, M., Bryant, R., Schenk, E., Amiri, S. (2016). Does nursing research matter? Student learning using validated EBP instruments. In Western Institute of Nursing's 49th Annual Communicating Nursing Research Conference, Anaheim, CA.

Wilson, M., Sleutel, M., Newcomb, P., Behan, D., Walsh, J., Wells, J. N., et al. (2015). Empowering nurses with evidence-based practice environments: Surveying magnet, pathway to excellence, and non-magnet facilities in one healthcare system. *Worldviews on Evidence-Based Nursing, 12*(1), 12–21. https://doi.org/10.1111/wvn.12077.

FURTHER READING

Johns Hopkins Medicine, Center for Evidence-Based Practice. (2017). *Johns Hopkins nursingevidence-based practice model.* Retrieved from: http://www.hopkinsmedicine.org/evidence-based-practice/jhn_ebp.html. (Accessed 05.21.17).

National Academies of Sciences, Engineering, & Medicine. (2012). *Activity: The learning-healthcare system in America.* Retrieved from: http://www.nationalacademies.org/hmd/Activities/Quality/LearningHealthCare.aspx. (Accessed 05.19.17).

Smith, M., Saunders, R., Stuckhardt, L., & McGinnis, J. M. (2013). *Best care at lower cost: The path to continuously learning health care in America.* Washington, D.C.: National Academies Press.

CHAPTER 2

Information as a Commodity

Loree Hyde

kpLibraries, Clackamas, OR, United States

In 1984 in Hackers, Steven Levy offered the "hacker ethic," upholding that "all information should be free: Linking directly with the principle of access, information needs to be free for hackers to fix, improve, and reinvent systems. A free exchange of information allows for greater overall creativity" (Levy, 1984, p. 27). He later credits Stuart Brand with this idea, and Brand, in his own consideration of these ethics, is famously quoted as saying that "information wants to be expensive, because it's so valuable" (Levy, 2014; Wagner, 2003). We continue to experience this juxtaposition today. In nursing, for example, information often takes the form of the scholarly works relied upon in evidenced-based practice. Its value can be determined by format, publisher, or the way in which it is used. In the seminal definition of evidence-based medicine, David Sackett refers to this concept as the "best available external clinical evidence from systematic research" (Sackett, Rosenberg, Gray, Haynes, & Richardson, 1996, p. 71). Although the adoption of evidence-based practice was seen as somewhat slow in coming to nursing, the use of information in this way has been shown to be highly valuable by saving nurses time, reducing adverse events, and changing practice (Marshall, Morgan, Klem, Thompson, & Wells, 2014).

2.1 FRAMEWORK FOR INFORMATION LITERACY FOR HIGHER EDUCATION

The statement that "information has value," as we see in the ACRL Framework for Information Literacy for Higher Education, is not hard to intellectualize in a variety of ways. Today we see "information warfare" causing conflicts across the globe, and the use of market information in business and industry can make or break an economy. This Frame recognizes the commodifying of information, as well as its "means to influence." It equally values information as a pathway through educational undertakings and as providing context and an informed perspective for understanding and moving through the world.

The legal and socioeconomic interests as noted in the Frame influence the production and dissemination of information in terms of intellectual property, a fundamental element of the creation of scholarly work (Association of College & Research Libraries [ACRL], 2016). Indeed, publishing models have become a harbinger of how information is valued. The reputation of a journal and its Impact Factor (Chodos, 2017) are starting to be valued less, as Open Access (OA) publishing models bring research more quickly to the community without the barrier of an expensive subscription. Unfortunately, this value can be subjugated, as OA publishing has been blighted with the practices of "predatory open-access (POA) journals that prioritize profit over the integrity of academic scholarship" and exploit the pay for publication or submission model in journals that, by design, are not reputable (Harzing & Adler, 2014). Access issues divide scholars and can have a tangible effect on the research process if research is completed but cannot be easily shared and used in the creation of new knowledge, the creative aspect that Levy identified. As methods of production and dissemination evolve, learners struggle with the concepts of intellectual property and copyright and the associated rules of attribution. The Frame represents the information literate learner as able to follow those rules, acknowledging and placing the appropriate value on the work of others. All of this comes after the recognition that access to information is not equal for all nurses. Those working in rural and other medically underserved areas may not be able to find and retrieve evidence due to socioeconomic factors such as lack of access to journal subscriptions, the internet, or even basic infrastructure.

OA publishing speeds up not only the publication cycle but also the creation of new knowledge by making research more accessible to others pursuing their own scholarly work (Right to Research Coalition, 2010). The increasing the rate at which research moves into practice is in its own right a measure of value in healthcare, exemplified in the practice of translational medicine. This rapidly growing discipline strives to accelerate the innovation of new diagnostic tools and therapies through a multidisciplinary "bench-to-bedside" approach (Woolf, 2008; Glasgow, Dunphy, & Mainous, 2011).

There is a need to embrace technology-infused education, transdisciplinary approaches to care, and translational research as today's students learn how to effectively assess and manage some of the most significant health problems currently confronting our society (e.g., mental health disorders, obesity, patient safety) and how to innovate changes in our health care system (Melnyk & Davidson, 2009).

Information being used as a means to influence is most evident in the creation of health policy. Because nurses comprise the majority of health personnel in many healthcare settings and are the clinicians closest to patient care, their participation in policymaking is paramount at all stages, ranging from local to organizational, state, national, and global levels (Shamian, 2016; Kunaviktikul, 2014).

A key message of the IOM report *The Future of Nursing* is that "nurses should practice to the full extent of their education and training" (Institute of Medicine [IOM], 2011, p. 4). As the identified physician shortage plays out (Kirch & Petelle, 2017), the need for nurses to practice at the top of their scope increases and should be reflected in nursing education. This holistic approach to practice early in a nurse's education will only be successful if they are able consume and utilize information effectively.

The value of personal information, per the Frame, should be carefully considered, particularly in an online setting. This becomes even more important in a healthcare environment where patient health information (PHI) has become a true commodity. Big data is big business, and the widespread adoption of the electronic health record (EHR) has made a vast supply of PHI accessible to researchers. Beyond clinical data, everything from costs of services, effects of pharmaceuticals, and even patient financial information can be gleaned from an EHR repository. While these data sets serve as a source of potential innovation in healthcare, they also provide information to guide competitive business practices and should be recognized as valuable in that way as well (Simpson, 2015).

Protection of PHI is another concern that indicates the value of this data. The Nursing & Midwifery Councils' publication, *The Code*, makes privacy a key component of their "Prioritize People" standard, asking nurses to "respect people's right to privacy and confidentiality… making sure that they are informed about their care and that information about them is shared appropriately" (Nursing and Midwifery Council, 2015, p. 6). Patient privacy is a principle value that must remain protected, as exemplified by HIPAA (Health Insurance Portability and Accountability Act of 1996) as well as the Patient's Bill of Rights (U.S. Centers for Medicare & Medicaid Services, 2010; Kayyali, Knott, & Van Kuiken, 2013; Simpson, 2015).

2.2 INFORMATION LITERACY COMPETENCY STANDARDS FOR NURSING (ILCSN)

Standard One of the ILCSN gives us the information literate nurse determining "the nature and extent of the information needed." Identifying the information need and the searching process are central to this Standard and are discussed later in Chapter Five, but here we also have the elucidation of the "nature" of information, which imparts value. For those familiar with evidence-based practice, one of the first related concepts to come to mind will be levels or guidelines for rating evidence, as defined in a variety of EBP nursing models, such as ACE Star, Iowa, Johns Hopkins, and Stetler (Schaffer, Sandau, & Diedrick, 2013). While the different models have their unique approaches, all agree that rigorous evaluation of how the research was produced is imperative in determining its value. Standard One of the ILCSN also highlights the process of information construction from data, leading to the creation of new knowledge (ACRL, 2013, p. 1).

A paucity of information on a topic can indicate a need for study in an area, making the scare literature that exists more valuable, as well as any new research that might be conducted to fill the gap. Standard Three, Performance Indicator 3 provides detailed outcomes on the construction of new knowledge. Of value in this process is the ability to recognize inter-relationships among concepts and combine them. Performance Indicator 4 tasks the nurse with comparing this "new knowledge with prior knowledge to determine the value added, contradictions, or other unique characteristics of the information" (ACRL, 2013, p. 3). Here the ILCSN guide the nurse to integrate new information, to consider practice changes, or to test theory or strategy, moving nursing research and practice forward. "New Knowledge, Innovations & Improvements" is also one of the 5 Model Components of the ANCC's Magnet© Recognition Program, the respected distinction a healthcare organization can receive for nursing excellence and high-quality patient care. The Magnet© framework for nursing practice and research em-phasizes creating "new models of care, application of existing evidence, new evidence, and visible contributions to the science of nursing" (American Nurses Credentialing Center, 2008). The creation of new knowledge is a key component in achieving Magnet© status, a designation that itself im-parts value by increasing the stature of a nursing enterprise.

Conversely, if a concept has an overabundance of published research, identifying publication types and levels of evidence will aid in determining value as well. Standard Three details how nurses should critically evaluate information and its sources, thus determining its value to them in their pur-suit of quality improvement, practicing from an evidence-base, and research. Performance Indicator 2 tells us that the nurse "selects information by ar-ticulating and applying criteria for evaluating both the information and its sources." Nurses should be able to emphasize and indicate value discovered in the critical appraisal of information and understand the impact of infor-mation from a variety of disciplines beyond nursing. Becoming skilled at critical appraisal provides the experience needed to understand the diversity of different types of information, from distinguishing fact from opinion, to discerning contextual factors, to identifying gaps in the literature. This is integral to building a nurse's unique knowledge base, a building block of their evidence-based practice.

We see a more traditional interpretation of the value of information considered in Standard Five of the ILCSN, which states, "the information literate nurse understands many of the economic, legal, and social issues surrounding the use of information and accesses and uses information ethically and legally." Adherence to copyright laws and regulations indicate an understanding of intellectual property and how attribution indicates varied types of value.

Here again we see the way information is published and accessed as indicators of value. Performance Indicator 1 in Standard Five identifies the complexities of different publishing models with an example of identifying and discussing "issues related to free vs. fee-based access to information" as a means of understanding the ethical, legal, and socioeconomic issues tied to information. Understanding the licensing restrictions and institutional policies regarding use of resources is highlighted in the standard as well as another indicator of value. Finally, PI-2, Outcome C, acknowledges that recognizing "the complexities of accessing full text and the various publishing models," one of the most valuable skills upon which evidence-based practice is built.

2.3 PROGRESSION OF NURSING EDUCATION AND PRACTICE

2.3.1 The Quality and Safety Education for Nurses (QSEN) Prelicensure

The Quality and Safety Education for Nurses (QSEN) Competencies illuminate the value inherent in the process of effectively managing information in healthcare by asking the nurse to "recognize the time, effort, and skill required for computers, databases and other technologies to become reliable and effective tools for patient care" (Cronenwett et al., 2007). QSEN defines Informatics as the nurse's use of "information and technology to communicate, manage knowledge, mitigate error, and support decision making" (Cronenwett et al., 2007). Information and related technology skills are crucial for quality, patient-centered care, and are put forth in the competencies as necessary attitudes for lifelong learning.

Privacy of patient data is also considered in the Informatics section of the QSEN Competencies, making its value apparent by the fact of its inclusion, as well as in the guiding documents being consulted in this work. As the electronic health record evolves, patient data grows in value, but the systems that form this fertile environment also make breaches of privacy a greater concern. If patients do not feel their privacy is protected, they may withhold information or avoid seeking care, threatening their welfare.

2.3.2 The Essentials of Baccalaureate Education for Professional Nursing Practice

The AACN Essentials of Baccalaureate Education for Professional Nursing Practice (EBE) make the critical appraisal of information within the evidence-based practice process foundational to professional practice. Baccalaureate graduates are asked to consider levels of evidence to aid in determining the quality of the research design and methodology, as well as relevance to patient care (American Association of Colleges of Nursing [AACN], 2008). Diversity of information is also valued in the *Essentials*. To provide informed care, nurses should also seek diverse, interprofessional perspectives from a variety of disciplines in all aspects of the care they provide (AACN, 2008).

In Essential VII: *Clinical Prevention and Population Health,* it is made clear that it is important for baccalaureate prepared nurses to recognize data as the information necessary to help them understand populations. Nurses involved in public health should analyze and employ epidemiological and demographic data to inform their work with the objective of influencing outcomes and advocating for health policy to improve the health of a community or group (AACN, 2008; Institute of Medicine, 2013).

The value of information is made more overt in the broader, social justice position of the AACN EBE (AACN, 2008), which portrays the baccalaureate prepared nurse as an ethical manager of "data, information, knowledge, and technology." This approach to information assets demonstrates an expectation of understanding of worth, particularly considering the description of their use to do everything from communicating effectively to providing safe and effective patient care. The EBE holds up adherence of HIPAA rules to safeguard patient health information as an example of these practices. The consideration of patient privacy and acknowledgement of its importance is clarified further in the *Essentials* which ask that baccalaureate nursing education will prepare a nurse to "uphold ethical standards related to data security, regulatory requirements confidentiality, and clients' right to privacy", including advocating for the protection of human subjects when conducting research (AACN, 2008).

This same section, *Professionalism and Professional Values*, brings not only moral and ethical weight to the use of information but also highlights "legal conduct" (AACN, 2008). When engaging with information, the nurse must recognize copyright and licensing restrictions as well as institutional policies regarding access to and use of resources. These protections are another indicator of the value of the information being utilized.

In its discussion of generalist nursing practice, the final *Essential* (IX) acknowledges the significance a scientific base of knowledge, including current evidence from research, plays in a nurse's role as "the human link between the patient and the complex healthcare environment" that includes wellness, health promotion, disease management, and care at the end of life. Graduates are expected to be lifelong learners, continually working to "translate, integrate and apply knowledge that leads to improvements in patient outcomes" (AACN, 2008, p. 30).

2.3.3 The Essentials of MASTER'S Education in Nursing

Diversity of information is valued at the Master's level of nursing education as well. In The Essentials of Master's Education in Nursing Essential I: *Background for Practice from Sciences and Humanities*, we see the masters-prepared nurse diversifying their use of information by integrating "findings from the sciences and the humanities, biopsychosocial fields, genetics, public health, quality improvement, health economics, translational science, and organizational sciences for the continual improvement of nursing care at the unit, clinic, home, or program level" (AACN, 2011, p. 9). Examples go beyond nursing theory and science and include a wide variety of information types, from economic models to the products of systems science and chaos theory.

In this advanced level of nursing education, we also come to a greater focus toward the consumption of data, with master's students monitoring trends in clinical data to better understand implications for changing nursing care (AACN, 2011). This information is assessed to develop strategies that diminish risk and improve health outcomes (AACN, 2011). Building upon the expectations of the baccalaureate nurse, the master's-prepared nurse also uses "statistical and epidemiological principles to synthesize data, information, and knowledge to evaluate and achieve optimal health outcomes" (AACN, 2011, p. 18). The master's prepared nurse is well positioned to not only skillfully manage that data but also move into roles as patient advocates and educators, assisting patients, students, caregivers, and healthcare professionals in accessing, understanding, evaluating, and applying evidence to practice (Norful, Swords, Marichal, Cho, & Poghosyan, 2017). Finally, the *Masters Essentials* carry over the concepts of "ethical and legal issues related to the use of information technology, including copyright, privacy, and confidentiality issues" (AACN, 2011, p. 20) as detailed in the EBE and the *ACRL Framework of Information Literacy*.

2.3.4 The Essentials of Doctoral Education for Advanced Nursing Practice

While the Doctor of Nursing Practice (DNP) is not primarily research focused, the use and value of information in evidence-based practice is exemplified by a focus on Translational Medicine, which includes a collaborative approach to analytically evaluating practice, solving problems, and improving outcomes (DePalma & McGuire, 2005; AACN, 2006). The foundational competencies in *The Essentials of Doctoral Education for Advanced Nursing Practice* (EDE) represent the DNP graduate engaged in critical appraisal of the research literature, as well as other evidence, to determine and implement best practice (AACN, 2006; Diers, 1995; EDE II). The DNP will also utilize information technology to garner information to inform budgeting and issues of productivity (AACN, 2006). As these skills are developed, the DNP graduate can "apply new knowledge, manage individual and aggregate level information, and assess the efficacy of patient care technology appropriate to a specialized area of practice" (AACN, 2006, p. 12). These providers will implement quality improvement projects and make administrative decisions based on their information gathering skills and understanding, as well as their knowledge of "standards and principles for selecting and evaluating information systems and patient care technology, and related ethical, regulatory, and legal issues" (AACN, 2006, p. 13). At the DNP level, the nurse is not only able to understand the ethical and legal issues surrounding the use of information but also to provide leadership to others in regard to the use of various types of information and systems.

With a practice entrenched in clinical prevention and population health, the DNP graduate can extract and analyze data from a wide variety of sources, including research in epidemiology, infectious diseases, disaster preparedness, and occupational and environmental health (AACN, 2006).

Public health nurses engage with this type of data in order to effect change in health culture across communities. In this vein, public health nurses "have been health advocates positively influencing the environments where people are born, grow, work, live, and age" for over 140 years (Levin et al., 2016).

Similar to the masters prepared nurse, the DNP synthesizes concepts but is now advancing from patient care, quality improvement and EBP, to evaluating interventions to "address health promotion/disease prevention efforts, improve health status/access patterns, and/or address gaps in care of individuals, aggregates, or populations (AACN, 2006). As these practitioners translate evidence and integrate new knowledge into nursing practice and beyond, it is easy to see how the diverse information involved drives these processes and establishes its value (Institute of Medicine, 2011). Doctoral requirements for independent projects and dissertations are important for building the capacity for DNPs to contribute to quality improvement and translational science, but they take time and commitment to scholarly approaches to inquiry.

2.4 THE RESEARCH-FOCUSED DOCTORAL PROGRAM IN NURSING: PATHWAYS TO EXCELLENCE

The ACCN Pathways to Excellence for the Research-Focused Doctoral Program in Nursing is a guiding document for Doctor of Philosophy (PhD) programs in Nursing. Its emphasis moves from mastering the concepts and understanding the information in nursing education, to the development of new knowledge and science. The PhD standards and recommendations assume a mastery of the EBE, at the very least, and through the *Expected Outcomes and curricular Elements of the PhD Programs in Nursing*, quickly move to a higher level of skill required for gaining the information necessary to develop nursing science. At the PhD level, graduates are expected to master in-depth knowledge in a selected area of research, incorporating related history, philosophy, and different science perspectives and creating a specialized knowledge base. These PhD prepared nurses will conduct original research, creating new knowledge and information that will influence policy, nursing practice and the profession. Throughout this process they will employ the appropriate methods of data, information and knowledge management, processing, and analysis. The outcomes expected for the PhD graduate are also the information, or scholarly works, required to educate the next generation of nurses, and expand the science of nursing (AACN, 2010).

APPENDIX 2.1. TEACHING TIPS

Nurse educators and nursing librarians can facilitate nursing students learning by using any of the following teaching tips (Health Sciences Interest Group, 2013):

- Discuss the various models of scientific publishing, including open-access journals. Explore publication and subscription fees for several journal titles. Examine sites such as PubMedCentral, BioMedCentral, PLoS, and DOAJ; identifies how such sites fit into the information cycle and publishing practices.
- Use a checklist to navigate fair use guidelines and determines whether a particular use of copyrighted information is appropriate. The Fair Use Checklist from Columbia University's Copyright Advisory Office (http://copyright.columbia.edu/copyright/fair-use/fair-use-checklist) is excellent, but it would be even better to develop a checklist specifically for the health professions.
- Highlight the ethical, legal, and financial issues of access to subscription databases and the use of material provided by institutions and organizations outside of the academic setting.
- Use examples to demonstrate correct citation of references, and practices reading citations from a variety of sources. Discuss the historical development of citation styles and how they demonstrate the values of the discipline they represent.
- Investigate and compare impact factors and altmetrics.

REFERENCES

American Association of Colleges of Nursing. (2006). *The essentials of doctoral education for advanced nursing practice.* Retrieved from http://www.aacn.nche.edu/dnp/Essentials.pdf.

American Association of Colleges of Nursing. 2008. *The essentials of baccalaureate education for professional nursing practice.* Retrieved from http://www.aacn.nche.edu/education-resources/BaccEssentials08.pdf Accessed 04.01.17.

American Association of Colleges of Nursing. (2010). *The research-focused doctoral program in nursing: Pathways to excellence.* Retrieved from http://www.aacn.nche.edu/education-resources/PhDPosition.pdf.

American Association of Colleges of Nursing. (2011). *The essentials of master's education in nursing.* Retrieved from http://www.aacn.nche.edu/education-resources/MastersEssentials11.pdf.

American Nurses Credentialing Center. (2008). *A new model for ANCC's magnet recognition program® [brochure].* Retrieved from http://www.nursecredentialing.org/documents/magnet/newmodelbrochure.aspx.

Association of College & Research Libraries. (2013). *The information literacy competency standards for nursing.* Retrieved from http://www.ala.org/acrl/standards/nursing.

Association of College & Research Libraries. (2016). *Framework for information literacy for higher education.* Retrieved from http://www.ala.org/acrl/sites/ala.org.acrl/files/content/issues/infolit/Framework_ILHE.pdf.

Chodos, A. (Ed.). 2017. Does the 'impact factor' impact decisions on where to publish? *APS News*. Retrieved from http://www.aps.org/publications/apsnews/200604/impact.cfm Accessed 5.12.17.

Cronenwett, L., Sherwood, G., Barnsteiner, J., Disch, J., Johnson, J., & Mitchell, P. (2007). Quality and safety education for nurses. *Nursing Outlook, 55*(3), 122–131.

DePalma, J.A., & McGuire, D. B. (2005). Research. In A. B. Hamric, J.A. Spross, & C. Hanson (Eds.), *Advanced practice nursing: An integrative approach* (3rd ed., pp. 257–300). Philadelphia, PA: Elsevier Saunders.

Diers, D. (1995). Clinical scholarship. *Journal of Professional Nursing, 11*(1), 24–30.

Glasgow, M., Dunphy, L., & Mainous, R. (2011). *Innovative nursing educational curriculum for the 21st century*. Report of the Committee on the Robert Wood Johnson Foundation Initiative on the Future of Nursing, at the Institute of Medicine. *The future of nursing: Leading change, advancing health*, Washington, D.C.: National Academies Press.

Harzing, A. W., & Adler, N. J. 2014. Disseminating knowledge: From potential to reality— New open-access journals collide with convention *Academy of Management Learning & Education*. Advance online publication. Retrieved from https://www.harzing.com/download/predatory.pdf Accessed 5.2.17.

Health Sciences Interest Group. (2013). *Teaching tips - Mapping to the ACRL information literacy competency standards for nursing*. Retrieved from https://healthsciencesinterestgroup. wikispaces.com/Teaching+Tips+-+Mapping+to+the+ACRL+Information+Literacy +Competency+Standards+for+Nursing. Accessed August 16, 2017.

Institute of Medicine. 2011. Report of the committee on the Robert Wood Johnson Foundation initiative on the future of nursing. *The future of nursing: Leading change, advancing health*, Washington, D.C.: National Academies Press.

Institute of Medicine. 2013. Report of the Board on Population Health and Public Health Practice, Committee on Quality Measures for the Healthy People Leading Health Indicators. (2013). *Toward quality measures for population health and the leading health indicators*, Washington, D.C.: The National Academies Press.

Kayyali, B., Knott, D., & Van Kuiken, S. (2013). *The 'big data' revolution in healthcare: Accelerating value and innovation*. Retrieved from http://www.mckinsey.com/industries/ healthcare-systems-and-services/our-insights/the-big-data-revolution-in-us-health-care.

Kirch, D. G., & Petelle, K. (2017). Addressing the physician shortage: The peril of ignoring demography. *Jama, 317*(19), 1947–1948. https://doi.org/10.1001/jama.2017.2714.

Kunaviktikul, W. (2014). Moving towards the greater involvement of nurses in policy development. *International Nursing Review, 61*(1), https://doi.org/10.1111/inr.12092.

Levin, P., Cooper, J., Jones, A., Stepanian, C. E., & Stanley, S. A. R. (2016). *The Public Health Nurse: Necessary Partner for the Future of Healthy Communities A Position Paper of the Association of Public Health Nurses*. Retrieved from http://phnurse.org/resources/ Documents/APHN-PHN%20Value-Position%20P_APPROVED%205.30.2016.pdf.

Levy, S. (1984). *Hackers : Heroes of the computer revolution* (1st ed.). Garden City, N.Y.: Anchor Press/Doubleday.

Levy, S. (2014). *Backchannel. "Hackers" and "Information Wants to Be Free"*. Retrieved from https://medium.com/backchannel.

Marshall, J. G., Morgan, J. C., Klem, M. L., Thompson, C. A., & Wells, A. L. (2014). The value of library and information services in nursing and patient care. *Online Journal of Issues in Nursing, 19*(3). https://doi.org/10.3912/OJIN.Vol19No03PPT02.

Melnyk, B., & Davidson, S. (2009). Creating a culture of innovation in nursing education through shared vision, leadership, interdisciplinary partnerships, and positive deviance. *Nursing Administration Quarterly, 33*(4). https://doi.org/10.1097/NAQ.0b013e3181b9dcf8.

Norful, A., Swords, K., Marichal, M., Cho, H., & Poghosyan, L. (2017). Nurse practitioner– physician comanagement of primary care patients: The promise of a new delivery care model to improve quality of care. *Advance online publication Health Care Management Review*, https://doi.org/10.1097/HMR.0000000000000161.

Nursing and Midwifery Council. (2015). *The Code for nurses and midwives.* Retrieved from https://www.nmc.org.uk/code.

Right to Research Coalition. (2010). *Why open access?* Retrieved from http://www.right-toresearch.org/learn/whyoa/index.shtml.

Sackett, D. L., Rosenberg, W. M. C., Gray, J. A. M., Haynes, R. B., & Richardson, W. S. (1996). Evidence based medicine: What it is and what it isn't. *British Medical Journal, 312*(7023), https://doi.org/10.1136/bmj.312.7023.71.

Schaffer, M. A., Sandau, K. E., & Diedrick, L. (2013). Evidence-based practice models for organizational change: Overview and practical applications. *Journal of Advanced Nursing, 69*(5), 1197–1209.

Shamian, J. (2016). In setting global policy, nursing's voice is needed. *The American Journal of Nursing, 116*(8), https://doi.org/10.1097/01.NAJ.0000490148.13877.f4.

Simpson, R. L. (2015). Big data and nursing knowledge. *Nursing Administration Quarterly, 39*(1), 87–89. https://doi.org/10.1097/naq.0000000000000076.

Wagner, R. P. (2003). Information wants to be free: Intellectual property and the mythologies of control. *Columbia Law Review, 103*(4), 995–1034.

Woolf, S. (2008). The meaning of translational research and why it matters. *JAMA, 299*(2), https://doi.org/10.1001/jama.2007.26.

U.S. Centers for Medicare & Medicaid Services, Center for Consumer Information & Insurance Oversight. (2010). *Patient's bill of rights.* Retrieved from https://www.cms.gov/CCIIO/Programs-and-Initiatives/Health-Insurance-Market-Reforms/Patients-Bill-of-Rights.html.

FURTHER READING

Palmer, I. S. 1986. The emergence of clinical scholarship as a professional imperative *Journal of Professional Nursing, 25*, 318–325. Retrieved from http://search.ebscohost.com/login.aspx?direct=true&db=c8h&AN=107553934&site=ehost-live Accessed 5.13.17.

CHAPTER 3

Format and Dissemination of Information

Loree Hyde
kpLibraries, Clackamas, OR, United States

As nurses gain skill in moving through the information seeking process they must consider how the resources they utilize were created and why. The methods in which scholarly works are created, published, and disseminated have changed dramatically in the last 20 years. While traditional resources such as books and journals have moved into the online environment, other forms of publishing have emerged. Now researchers publish data sets online to encourage transparency and reuse. Blog posts, wikis, and Tweets have become important to scholarly conversations in impactful and accelerated ways. While traditional research is currently the mainstay for nursing students, it is important to understand that as formats evolve, research advances more quickly and changes practice, thus increasing the importance of the consideration of evidence and its lifecycle. At the same time, nurses must consider their most effective avenues of communication around patient care to best meet the information needs of nurse colleagues, those in other disciplines and those they care for.

3.1 FRAMEWORK FOR INFORMATION LITERACY FOR HIGHER EDUCATION

Within the *ACRL Framework for Information Literacy for Higher Education*, "Information Creation as a Process" is the frame most concerned with the format and dissemination methods used to share information, and how those factors affect use and the message conveyed. A classic evidence-based practice example would be the consideration of a question as background or foreground, with background questions relying on more established ideas, typically found in review articles or textbooks and foreground questions more at the cutting edge of clinical research, answered by more complex research studies such as randomized controlled trials and systematic reviews (Aslam and Emmanuel, 2010). In nursing, qualitative research is highly applicable to the clinical setting as well and is useful in exploring cultural and social aspects of living with illness, pain, or disability, as well as providing professional and patient-centered perspectives on care and treatment (Holloway and Galvin, 2016). Some investigations may require consulting the primary data related from qualitative research, such as surveys, letters and interviews, or data sets from quantitative research (Association of College & Research Libraries [ACRL], 2013).

Grey literature from government agencies or professional organizations, such as study protocols, trail registries, conference proceedings, theses, dissertations, or white papers, may be the most appropriate format to provide contextual information or uncover innovation in practice. Grey literature may also reveal studies with null findings, which are impactful, yet "less likely to be published in peer-reviewed journals" (Adams et al., 2016).

Formats that take use into consideration are bountiful in the health sciences. At times, a meta-analysis or systematic review found searching MEDLINE or CINAHL may be the most appropriate resource, for example, in an educational setting. In practice, a short monograph from UpToDate or DynaMed on the same topic, linked from the electronic health record, would meet the nurse's need. While both have their origins in the synthesis of information, the resulting products are distinctly different, due to their intended use, and are designed to be accessed in the way that is most appropriate for the situation.

The Framework operationalizes consideration of creation processes with "Knowledge Practices" and "Dispositions" which ask the nurse to understand and speak to strengths and weaknesses when determining which format and manner of delivery is the best fit for a specific discipline or context. It is important for nurses to understand when a format is appropriate and how it will be perceived in use, e.g., is the platform stable or somewhat impermanent, as web-based publications can be. Or, in the case of statistical data, an understanding of data gathering may be necessary, such as the cycles that frame the US Census.

When seeking information, the nurse, now more than ever, is presented with a wide range of possible formats and distribution methods to contemplate. Scholarly communication continues to evolve and change with new formats appearing in response to a growing diversity of contexts and needs. Today we see the use of altmetrics alongside traditional measures of scientific impact such as citation analysis, impact factors, and levels of evidence (O'Connor et al., 2017). Communities of scholarship now have the option to consider blog posts, Tweets, and other social media and web-born publications.

Peer review may not only be in place for these publications (e.g., peer-reviewed blogs) but also beyond the traditional prepublication process and outside of editorials, and instead in the comments section of a blog post or a listserv, or on open platforms such as ScienceOpen, PubMed Commons, ResearchGate, PaperHive, and PubPeer (Tennant, 2017). Nurses will learn to tolerate, and appreciate ambiguity, and see the value in these developing formats.

As nurses move from novice to expert, they will develop their own methods for information creation and dissemination, with the same understanding of how their choices influence the information revealed in their creation and its use (ACRL, 2016). Nurses may generate any of many publication types and information products, from chart notes to randomized controlled trials to practice guidelines. One rapidly growing type of research with a unique creation process is Translational Medicine (TM) or Research. Translational Medicine is defined as transforming "scientific findings or discoveries from basic laboratory, clinical, or population studies into new clinical tools, processes or applications." The Translational Research method leverages team science with the goal of moving research more quickly from the "bench to the bedside," making new therapies more readily available (What is translational medicine?, 2017). TM differs in its in production in that rather than moving in a linear direction, it is described as "a robust and dynamic process involving bidirectional stages and complex feedback loops" (Grady, 2010, p. 164).

Examples of disciplines working alongside biomedicine and nursing are computational science, physics, genomics, and materials science. As the field progresses, new tools are required, for example, to deal with increasingly large data sets. New journals, such as the *Journal of Translational Medicine*, *Science Translational Medicine,* and *Translational Science and Evidence-Based Healthcare*, have started publication to support moving this research into practice.

3.2 INFORMATION LITERACY COMPETENCY STANDARDS FOR NURSING (ILCSN)

Within *The Information Literacy Competency Standards for Nursing*, Standard Two addresses effective and efficient access of information, which leads the nurse to consider format and method of dissemination in relation to where the information may be located. The retrieval system or systems housing the information need to be investigated, along with the development of search strategies, to discover the information within. Utilization of controlled vocabularies and database functionality will play a part in access as well. The nurse may search in mainstream and specialized databases, directories, library catalogs and use several search engines. As grey literature is considered, so are the challenges encountered when accessing it, as discoverability is often not a straightforward path. Grey literature is not widely disseminated and is most often made available outside of commercial publishing on government and association web sites, in institutional repositories, and via other the web-based and ephemeral venues such as blogs, microblogs, wikis, listservs, and even podcasts (Giustini, 2012).

Other aspects of access for the nurse searcher to consider are utilizing available systems such as link resolvers and interlibrary loan to locate full text, and online or in-person services, including library staff or even reaching out to primary investigators (ACRL, 2013). Management of retrieved resources in relation to their creation process can be important as well. Grouping similar resources together can add to their collective value and illuminate a progression of research with relevance and utility. Throughout the creation process the nurse will apply appropriate technologies to organize, collaborate, and communicate, and may participate in the use, selection, and design of systems that support evidence-based practice, such as institutional repositories. Ultimately the nurse may use a variety of information types, including patient and public health information, scholarly papers, workplace reports, blogs, and materials for teaching.

Standard Four of *The Information Literacy Competency Standards for Nursing* helps to put this frame into perspective, as it asks the nurse to think about format and methods of dissemination in the effective use of information for a specific purpose (ACRL, 2013). As a nurse goes through the creation process they apply new and prior knowledge, organizing content to support intended use, and for the format required (e.g., poster, paper; care plan, practice guideline, procedure, or patient instruction) (ACRL, 2013). At the highest level, this may mean conducting original research, which could include the incorporation of raw data, quotations, paraphrasings, and/or images to support the purpose of the final product. As is typical, in research and literature searching, the methods may need to be revised as the nurse moves through the creation process. Should the nurse be investigating a practice change, initiating that change could be the final output, which would also require assessment and possible revision.

3.3 PROGRESSION OF NURSING EDUCATION AND PRACTICE

3.3.1 The Quality and Safety Education for Nurses (QSEN) Prelicensure

In their support of patient-centered care, the prelicensure nurse must find ways to communicate patient values to the healthcare team (Cronenwett, 2007). This foundational element of evidence-base practice may take place in varying formats, from charting in the electronic health record to report out in interdisciplinary rounds, hand-offs, and huddles, to care coordination planning (Gausvik et al., 2015). Structured nursing communication on interdisciplinary acute care teams improves perceptions of safety, efficiency, understanding of care planning and teamwork, as well as job satisfaction. Processes of care can also be shared via more visual formats, such as flow-charts or cause and effect diagrams, or checklists to decrease reliance on memory. As nurses promote their own perspectives about patient care in their communications, their professional opinions are a component of format as well. To minimize risk of errors or hazards, the nurse must be sensitive in the way they form their communications to best serve the needs of the patient and the care team throughout all transitions of care. For all information created around patient care to be shared effectively, nurses should work continually to improve their communication, as well as the systems and information management tools used to document and monitor outcomes and support effective teamwork (Cronenwett et al., 2007).

Evidence-based practice gives the prelicensure nurse the opportunity to consider format and dissemination of information as they consult the literature related to clinical practice and demonstrate their knowledge of scientific methods and processes. They must determine what types of publications best suit the populations they serve and meet their information needs. If considering the effects of an intervention on a population, they will need to move beyond a case study in the evidence and seek observational studies with larger sample sizes. If they are interested in quality of life, they will want to read qualitative literature rather than looking for randomized controlled trials, which may be the perfect type of study to reveal the effectiveness of a therapy or drug (see Chapter Six—*Type of Study for Question* chart for more on this topic). Once the nurse has determined what type of information they need and where to access it, they may then move to integrate newfound evidence into their standards of practice or put it to use in quality improvement projects (Cronenwett et al., 2007).

3.3.2 The Essentials of Baccalaureate Education for Professional Nursing Practice

The Essentials of Baccalaureate Education for Professional Nursing Practice (EBE) asks that nurses demonstrate an understanding of the basic elements of the research process as well as skill in using information systems to obtain evidence for their own benefit and clinical practice (American Association of Colleges of Nursing [AACN], 2008). A nurse in the Baccalaureate phase of their education should develop knowledge of the different formats in which information is created and know where to look for information at different stages of the research process. These nurses will come to recognize levels of evidence as represented by publication types such as "textbooks, case studies, reviews of literature, research critiques, controlled trials, evidence-based clinical practice guidelines, meta-analysis, and systematic reviews" (AACN, 2008, p. 17). Nurses will learn what repositories hold different forms of information, be it library catalogs, bibliographic databases, point of care tools, or websites. They will use search strategies in bibliographic databases such as CINAHL and MEDLINE to locate relevant research. Employing limiters and using controlled vocabularies, such as CINAHL headings and Medical Subject Headings (MeSH) terms alongside keywords in the search process (and understanding the utility of each), should be included in the set of skills developed around accessing information. In addition, establishing saved searches and alerts automates and facilitates accessibility to new literature, setting the nurse up for continued access into the future. This necessary skill set for information retrieval also includes identifying and utilizing other sources of evidence such as point of care tools, some grey literature, and textbooks. Finally, managing information using reference management tools gives the Baccalaureate prepared nurse access to their own repository to have at hand through their educational program and into practice.

Baccalaureate-prepared nurses will consider format further when creating their own information products. They are encouraged to use "written, verbal, nonverbal, and emerging technology methods to communicate effectively" (AACN, 2008, p. 12). Like the prelicensure nurse they not only will participate in communication around patient care and evidence-based practice but will also create educational and practice resources, such as presentations, posters, papers, patient education, practice guidelines, and procedures. The nurse should consider the message being conveyed and how it will be delivered when designating a format for their product.

3.3.3 The Essentials of Master's Education in Nursing

The masters-prepared nurse will have a more strategic approach to access and a greater understanding of how information is disseminated. They will explore the hierarchies within controlled vocabularies, use scope notes, subheading, and be skilled at combining keywords with subject headings to build comprehensive searches, documenting their processes and continually working to improve them (AACN, 2011). These nurses will have more familiarity with grey literature as well. They will use citation tracking tools, along with their own managed collection of information, to track the historic origins of a given topic's scholarly conversation (AACN, 2008). The nurse at this level of education will also focus on retrieving outcome data to support decision-making around patient care. When evaluating the information retrieved, masters-prepared nurses are able to appraise (Saines et al., 2016), rather than format alone, to determine value and understand the limits of the information, based on how it was created.

The masters nurse identifies gaps where evidence is lacking and synthesizes information to address those deficiencies, addressing the needs of varied and diverse populations. Outcome data is also important to this process, as the nurse engages in translational research and employs statistical and epidemiological principles to synthesize those data to create new evidence for use in guiding the implementation of interventions that aim to improve patient care. As noted earlier, this can be a cyclical process, as interventions are evaluated and new questions are identified (AACN, 2011). The nurse will consider a variety of audiences when creating educational programs, policy, procedure, practice guidelines, etc. They will also select from different information and communication technologies for diffusion, determining what will be most effective in advancing patient education, enhancing accessibility of care, analyzing practice patterns, and improving outcomes, specifically those that are nurse sensitive, such as pressure ulcers, falls, and healthcare-associated infections (AACN, 2011).

3.3.4 The Essentials of Doctoral Education for Advanced Nursing Practice

Doctoral programs in Nursing Practice build on traditional master's programs "by providing education in evidence-based practice, quality improvement, and systems leadership, among other key areas" (AACN, 2006, p. 10). Graduates of Doctor of Nursing Practice (DNP) programs will have advanced searching skills, employing strategies such as adjacency searching and using field codes to create systematic searches to access information, not only for the appraisal of outcomes of care but also of healthcare programs and systems (AACN, 2006). These nurses are correspondingly valued as experts in guiding the design of databases that "generate meaningful evidence for nursing practice" and are skilled in evaluating methods of distribution (AACN, 2006).

As a practitioner and researcher, the DNP will use their technological skills in identifying gaps in the literature and explore the feasibility of generating, collecting, and aggregating primary data to answer research and practice questions (AACN, 2006). Even more so, the DNP focuses on collaborating on translational research projects to apply research findings directly to patient care. As part of the groundwork for the dynamic and iterative process of implementing research, the DNP will interrogate the format to assess the suitability of evidence (Saines et al., 2016; AACN, 2006). Throughout this process the DNP will consider appropriate format when leveraging their leadership skills to apply new knowledge and bring evidence-based practice recommendations to clinical decision-making, program evaluation, policy development, quality improvement, and education within their communities of practice (Stevens, 2005).

3.4 THE RESEARCH-FOCUSED DOCTORAL PROGRAM IN NURSING: PATHWAYS TO EXCELLENCE

The PhD in nursing will have the same complex skill set as the DNP for accessing evidence and understanding distribution models but will have had more opportunity to apply those skills, and thus have advanced expertise. The PhD nurse will endeavor to produce new data and knowledge, typically related to health outcomes, using traditional research methodologies which may include qualitative research, but are more likely to be efficacy studies such as the peer reviewed, randomized controlled trial (Vincent et al., 2011; Stevens, 2005). These nurses must consider formats beyond study types when disseminating research findings, as they may need to communicate implications for policy and nursing practice beyond their professional audiences, to other disciplines or the community. Grant applications are another format the PhD must concern themselves with as well, as securing funding is often the first step in creating evidence.

APPENDIX 3.1. TEACHING TIPS

Nurse educators and nursing librarians can facilitate nursing students learning by using any of the following teaching tips (Health Sciences Interest Group, 2013):

Discuss the publication cycle including the kind of information found at different stages of the cycle. Evaluate the credibility of each source. Identify examples of an informal medical website, a formal medical website, a medical blog, and medical databases.
- Define primary sources of nursing and shows an example of each.
- Define secondary sources of nursing and shows an example of each.
- Visit the library collection, find, and discuss content of nursing manuals, handbooks, etc., relevant to their field.
- Create two lists—one of different research populations and one of research methods. Distinguish which methods are appropriate for each of the listed populations.
- Evaluate medical databases identifying the content, scope, search functionality, etc.

REFERENCES

Adams, J., Hillier-Brown, F. C., Moore, H. J., Lake, A. A., Araujo-Soares, V., White, M., & Summerbell, C. (2016). Searching and synthesising 'grey literature' and 'grey information' in public health: Critical reflections on three case studies. *Systematic Reviews, 5*(1) https://doi.org/10.1186/s13643-016-0337-y.

Aslam, S., & Emmanuel, P. (2010). Formulating a researchable question: A critical step for facilitating good clinical research. *Indian Journal of Sexually Transmitted Diseases and AIDS, 31*(1), 47–50. https://doi.org/10.4103/0253-7184.69003.

American Association of Colleges of Nursing. (2006). *The essentials of doctoral education for advanced nursing practice.* Retrieved from http://www.aacn.nche.edu/dnp/Essentials.pdf.

American Association of Colleges of Nursing. (2008). *The essentials of baccalaureate education for professional nursing practice.* Retrieved from http://www.aacn.nche.edu/education-resources/BaccEssentials08.pdf.

American Association of Colleges of Nursing. (2011). *The essentials of master's education in nursing.* Retrieved from http://www.aacn.nche.edu/education-resources/MastersEssentials11.pdf.

Association of College & Research Libraries. (2013). *The information literacy competency standards for nursing.* Retrieved from http://www.ala.org/acrl/standards/nursing.

Association of College & Research Libraries. (2016). *Framework for information literacy for higher education.* Retrieved from http://www.ala.org/acrl/sites/ala.org.acrl/files/content/issues/infolit/Framework_ILHE.pdf.

Cronenwett, L., Sherwood, G., Barnsteiner, J., Disch, J., Johnson, J., Mitchell, P., & Warren, J. (2007). Quality and safety education for nurses. *Nursing Outlook, 55*(3), 122–131.

Gausvik, C., Lautar, A., Miller, L., Pallerla, H., & Schlaudecker, J. (2015). Structured nursing communication on interdisciplinary acute care teams improves perceptions of safety, efficiency, understanding of care plan and teamwork as well as job satisfaction. *Journal of Multidisciplinary Healthcare, 8*. https://doi.org/10.2147/JMDH.S72623.

Giustini, D. (2012). *Finding the hard to finds: Searching for grey literature [SlideShare slides]*. Retrieved from https://www.slideshare.net/giustinid/finding-the-hard-to-finds-searching-for-grey-gray-literature-2010.

Grady, P. (2010). Translational research and nursing science. *Nursing Outlook, 58*(3), https://doi.org/10.1016/j.outlook.2010.01.001.

Health Sciences Interest Group. (2013). *Teaching tips—Mapping to the ACRL information literacy competency standards for nursing*. Retrieved from https://healthsciencesinterestgroup.wikispaces.com/Teaching+Tips+-+Mapping+to+the+ACRL+Information+Literacy+Competency+Standards+for+Nursing. Accessed August 16, 2017.

Holloway, I., & Galvin, K. (2016). *Qualitative research in nursing and healthcare* (4th ed.). Hoboken: Wiley.

O'Connor, E. M., Nason, G. J., O'Kelly, F., Manecksha, R. P., & Loeb, S. (2017). Newsworthiness versus scientific impact: Are the most highly cited urology papers the most widely disseminated in the media? *BJU International.* Accepted Article https://doi.org/10.1111/bju.13881.

Saines, S. B. K., Intrator, M., Schmillen, H., & Wochna, L. (2016). *Rubrics for information literacy in higher education: ACRL frameworks [Working document]*. Retrieved from https://ohio.app.box.com/s/6ibteg78nrhrd4p9qg6re9vvk04jetko.

Stevens, K. R. (2005). *Essential competencies for evidence-based practice in nursing*. San Antonio, TX: Academic Center for Evidence-Based Practice.

Tennant, J. (2017, March 30). *What are the barriers to post-publication peer review? [Web log comment]*. Retrieved from http://blog.scienceopen.com/2017/03/what-are-the-barriers-to-post-publication-peer-review/#more-2748.

Vincent, D., Johnson, C., Velasquez, D., & Rigney, T. (2011). *DNP-prepared nurses as practitioner-researchers: Closing the gap between research and practice*. Retrieved from http://www.doctorsofnursingpractice.org/wp-content/uploads/2014/08/Vincet_et_al.pdf.

What is translational medicine? (2017). *Science Translational Medicine.* Retrieved from http://www.sciencemag.org/site/marketing/stm/definition.xhtml.

FURTHER READING

American Association of Colleges of Nursing. (2010). *The research-focused doctoral program in nursing: Pathways to excellence.* Retrieved from http://www.aacn.nche.edu/education-resources/PhDPosition.pdf.

American Association of Colleges of Nursing. (2016). *DNP fact sheet: The doctor of nursing practice.* Retrieved from http://www.aacn.nche.edu/media-relations/fact-sheets/dnp.

CHAPTER 4

The Conversation of the Scholars

Sue F. Phelps

Washington State University, Vancouver, WA, United States

Imagine that you enter a parlor. You come late. When you arrive, others have long preceded you, and they are engaged in a heated discussion, a discussion too heated for them to pause and tell you exactly what it is about. In fact, the discussion had already begun long before any of them got there, so that no one present is qualified to retrace for you all the steps that had gone before. You listen for a while, until you decide that you have caught the tenor of the argument; then you put in your oar. Someone answers; you answer him; another comes to your defense; another aligns himself against you, to either the embarrassment or gratification of your opponent, depending upon the quality of your ally's assistance. However, the discussion is interminable. The hour grows late, you must depart. And you do depart, with the discussion still vigorously in progress.

Burke (1941)

Kenneth Burke, a philosopher and rhetorician, introduced this metaphor for the "Unending Conversation" that has been often cited to illustrate scholarly discourse. This discourse is as true for nursing scholarship as it is for philosophers and it applies to all levels of nursing and nursing education. Though research and scholarship is certainly the focus of doctoral programs in nursing, the conversation of nursing scholars is associated with all levels of nursing education and through all nursing specialties. When fully understood, it makes sense out of the vast amounts of scholarly material with conflicting outcomes and ideas, and gives structure to the kinds of information seeking that spans decades of publications.

The conversation of nursing scholars dates back to 1859 when Florence Nightingale published "Notes on Nursing: What it is and what it is not" (1859). Her goal in writing this book was to share her ideas on how to best care for those needing medical care based on her experience in caring for the sick and injured. Nightingale advocated for systematic inquiry to improve health care practices but during that time in history she was ignored by the hospital training schools where nursing education was taking place (University of Maryland). According to Nay (2003), historically, much of nursing practice has been informed by tradition and provider preference rather than based on research evidence. Nursing research emerged, as we know it, when the Health Research Extension Act of 1985 became law and the National Center for Nursing Research (NCNR) at the National Institute of Health (NIH) was established in 1986 (Cantelon, 2010). To achieve their mission of improved health for individuals, communities, and families the "NINR supports and conducts clinical and basic research and research training on health and illness, research that spans and integrates the behavioral and biological sciences, and that develops the scientific basis for clinical practice" (NINR, 2016). Improvement in health care is the central theme in the conversation among nurses and nursing scholars.

4.1 FRAMEWORK FOR INFORMATION LITERACY FOR HIGHER EDUCATION

The Association of College and Research Libraries' (ACRL) Framework for Information Literacy for Higher Education (Framework) expresses Burke's metaphor in the frame titled *Scholarship as Conversation* saying "Communities of scholars, researchers, or professionals engage in sustained discourse with new insights and discoveries occurring over time as a result of varied perspectives and interpretations" (ACRL, 2016). In an editorial for Clinical Nurse Specialist Janet S. Fulton (2015) discusses the publication of peer-reviewed material by scientists with data gleaned from their research and by clinicians from practice applications to move nursing science forward. She reminds readers that the process is full of false starts and blind alleys but encourages the publication of all efforts in the pursuit of scientific knowledge, including studies that have disappointing outcomes. The sharing of failed research or research that did not have a positive outcome is necessary to the scholarly conversation among a community interested in solving a problem (Fulton, 2015). Fulton (2015) also introduces the idea that nurses at all levels of practice and education can contribute to the conversation. By including practicing nurses in scholarship there is the added benefit of bringing scientific findings closer to implementation in practice.

More recent publications indicate that nursing is moving toward closing the gap between research and practice by emphasizing the importance of clinical scholarship and the scholarship of application (Limoges, Acorn, & Osborne, 2015). The scholarship of application concept is in agreement with Fulton (2015) and the *Scholarship as Conversation* Frame in that they recognize "novice learners and experts at all levels can take part in the conversation" and that "new forms of scholarly and research conversations provide more avenues in which a wide variety of individuals may have a voice in the conversation" (ACRL, 2016). The scholarship of application is an expanded view of scholarship (scholarly conversation) that is beyond the domain of discovery and extended to knowledge application in community and service activities with the outcomes to benefit the larger community (Limoges et al., 2015). Nurses can put in their oar into the scholarly conversation at the level of original research and offer knowledge and discoveries at the bedside or in community practice.

Nurse leaders, who are registered nurses with advanced knowledge, can identify areas in which practice can be improved but need to go through a supervisor or formal leader to promote change. As the Frame points out "established power and authority structures may influence their ability to participate (in this case the practicing nurse) and can privilege certain voices and information" (ACRL, 2016).

Nurses wishing to enter into scholarly discourse can seek out conversations in their research area in a variety of venues and formats and therefore see themselves as someone who can add to the conversation (ACRL, 2016). Informal conversations can take place in blogs, wikis, via learning management systems, and in the workplace and classroom discussions. Fulton (2015) points out that publishing is not the only way to engage in scholarly conversation. She encourages writing letters to the editor of nursing publications as a way to contribute perspectives as well as to seek clarification for missing or unclear information.

Research is published by nursing scholars in journals and presented at conferences, however; practitioners can publish outcomes via a newsletter, through course completion assignments, or through a formal published paper. Limoges et al. (2015) stresses that knowledge production by academics and practitioners through the scholarship of application builds bridges between research, practice, and education as well as creates supportive management and leadership structures. In whatever form it takes, scholarly conversation is necessarily discursive as "ideas are formulated, debated, and weighed against one another over extended periods of time" (ACRL, 2016).

One barrier to scholarly conversation to support evidence-based practice in the nursing field is the occurrence of horizontal violence and subsequent lack of psychological safety in the workplace. Sometimes called workplace bullying this behavior appears frequently in nursing literature and has persisted since it was first identified 20 years ago (Brown & McCormack, 2016; Myers et al., 2016). Horizontal violence is described as aggressive behaviors including gossip, verbal abuse, intimidation, sarcasm, elitist attitudes, and body language toward individuals by one or more others and involves nurses, physicians, and patient families (Myers et al., 2016). The severity of the problem is such that the American Nurses Association issued a position statement in July 2015 articulating the responsibility of nurses and employers to "create and sustain a culture of respect, free of incivility, bullying and workplace violence" (ANA, 2015).

The current culture affects the self-esteem and confidence of nurses and impairs communication that otherwise might address improvements in clinical practice. Nurse Managers are called to change the culture and intervene when aggressive behaviors occur but there is little research on what works in which settings (Brown & McCormack, 2016). Educators in nursing and library science are advised to be mindful of this situation when discussing student nurses' stepping into the workplace and attempting to introduce change.

4.2 INFORMATION LITERACY COMPETENCY STANDARDS FOR NURSING

In the listening stage of "the endless conversation" the scholar identifies the elements of the question under discussion and considers what has been reported in previous research. Standard Three of the Information Literacy Competency Standards for Nursing (ILCSN) states "The information literate nurse critically evaluates the procured information and its sources, and as a result, decides whether or not to modify the initial query and/or seek additional sources and whether to develop a new research process." In doing so, they consider resources from a variety of disciplines; recognize interrelationships among concepts; and synthesize divergent information to answer a research question. They include information that is significant even when it contradicts current beliefs, procedures, and individual value systems in order to maintain a neutral position and an open mind (ACRL, 2013). When reading any given scholarly work they understand that it does not express the definitive perspective on the issue (ACRL, 2016) but only one voice in the conversation.

Standard Four indicates "The information literate nurse, individually or as a member of a group, uses information effectively to accomplish a specific purpose" (ACRL, 2013). Though nurses value the need for improvements in practice based on new knowledge they recognize that there are valid and invalid reasons to modify practice. Having attended to the conversation on a given issue, the nurse considers the content of the information collected to gain understanding of the view of the scholars and how it has progressed over time. The nurse must critically evaluate the literature they have found including research methodologies, interpretation of data, supporting arguments, and how the information compares to information from other sources. In doing so, they assess reliability, validity, accuracy, authority, currency, and bias. They sort facts from opinion and recognize manipulation of the information or its use. Additionally, the nurse considers the cultural, historical, physical, political, and social context within which the information was created or interpreted.

Having listened to the scholars and considered the information the nurse contributes to the scholarly conversation, moving it forward by adding individual analysis. At first they synthesize the ideas they have gathered to construct new concepts for themselves. Then, recognizing that existing information can be combined with original thought, experiments, or analysis the nurse can construct new concepts to add to the conversation. They can compare prior knowledge to new knowledge and determine contradictions or value that has been added and create an information product.

Whether that product is a poster, paper; care plan, practice guideline, procedure, or patient instruction they communicate the product effectively to others as they articulate to a variety of audiences the evidence base for practice decisions. The nurse may initiate change in performance of patient care when information or evidence indicates improvement in patient outcomes or decreased adverse events. Nurses also conduct original research studies to address gaps in the literature and produce information to address identified gaps, engaging in continuous improvement processes based on translational research skills to improve patient care.

With nurses, as within scholarly conversation in every discipline, there is agreement and disagreement. As an example, among the patients who are treated by nurses there has been a long standing controversy regarding vaccinations for children in England and the United States. Though much of the controversy has been between health care workers and parents influenced by nonmedical sources, there are also alternative health care providers that agree with the antivaccine movement. Additionally, within the scientific community there is debate regarding whether vaccinations should be mandatory. As stated by Tafuria et al. (2014) "scientific, cultural, and social points of view are hotly debated." When faced with such controversy the information literate nurse initiates and facilitates professional discourse and discussions as a team member, mentor, practitioner, preceptor, and/or educator. They seek expert opinion through a variety of mechanisms (e.g., interviews, electronic communication) and share evidence of best practices with interprofessional teams, professional association discussion lists, networks, and at professional conferences. They validate understanding and interpretation of the information through discourse with other individuals, subject-area experts, and/or practitioners and participate in classroom and virtual/electronic discussions. They determine probable accuracy by questioning the source of the information, limitations of the information gathering tools or strategies, and the reasonableness of the conclusions (ACRL, 2013). Only then can the nurse aid their patient in decision-making regarding a health issue.

4.3 PROGRESSION OF NURSING EDUCATION AND PRACTICE

4.3.1 The Quality and Safety Education for Nurses—Prelicensure

The Quality and Safety Education for Nurses (QSEN) targets competencies for prelicensure education on patient-centered care; teamwork and cooperation; and evidence-based practice. Scholarship for the prelicensed nurse focuses mainly on consuming information to carry out the practical tasks of nursing. Evidence-based practice for the prelicensed nurse requires that they "read original research and evidence reports related to an area of practice" (Cronenwett et al., 2007) in order to apply that information to patient care. The prelicensure nurse is expected to "integrate multiple dimensions of patient centered care" (Cronenwett et al., 2007) which includes understanding of information, education, research, clinical expertise, patient preference, and diversity of culture as they all contribute to patient and family values.

In order to work effectively as a team member each nurse needs to be able to function competently within their own strengths and limitations while soliciting input from other team members. The goal for the individual nurse is to be able to assert a position in discussions about patient care and ultimately build consensus and resolve conflict regarding patient interventions (Cronenwett et al., 2007). In order to present an informed opinion nurses can seek instruction from the literature published about the specific issue.

As a knowledgeable consumer of scholarship the prelicensed nurse is encouraged to question the rationale for practices that do not produce desired results or that have negative effects as well as analyzing errors for systems improvements. With appropriate channels of communication a practicing nurse can also raise questions that have not been addressed in the literature and trigger research. They are "ideally situated to identify areas requiring additional knowledge or understanding for quality patient care" (Limoges & Acorn, 2016).

4.3.2 The Essentials of Baccalaureate Education for Professional Nursing Practice

Baccalaureate graduates address the conversation of scholars from the perspective of competence in reading and evaluating the literature; integrating evidence into practice; and dissemination of knowledge to other nurses. Having been introduced to various methodologies used in research reports the baccalaureate nurse is able to differentiate between clinical opinion and research or evidence summaries. They analyze research articles by noticing whether the methodology is the best choice to answer the research question; the characteristics and the treatment of the sample groups; and the evaluation of the outcomes (Supporting Clinical Care, 2016).

Additionally, the baccalaureate nurse determines if a potential bias is present by recognizing if the research is sponsored by an industry or company with a special interest in the outcome. Furthermore they understand the political, historical, and social context around information creation (AACN, 2008).

As with the prelicensed nurses, baccalaureate nurses use scholarship to update their clinical knowledge and integrate reliable evidence to inform their practice and make clinical judgments. Knowing that research is constantly evolving baccalaureate graduates are expected to engage in lifelong learning and to share evidence of best practices with their interprofessional team.

4.3.3 The Essentials of Master's Education in Nursing

Masters graduates display a stronger focus on research and scholarship. At this level of education and practice the nurse is able to conduct a literature review or to participate in a systematic review to synthesize research to guide nursing practice. They are able to locate data from organizations and government repositories (US Census data, the National Center for Health Statistics, the Center for Disease Control and Prevention, state and county websites) and analyze that data (SPSS, Excel, AtlasTi). They are also able to interpret the data to address a specific research question.

Masters graduates assess the conversation of the scholars to determine what evidence is meaningful for nursing practice taking into consideration the reliability of the research and cultural principles. This may also include investigating political, historical, and social context around information creation. With influence and responsibility beyond the bedside, masters nurses "synthesize broad ecological, global and social determinants of health; principles of genetics and genomics; and epidemiologic data to design and deliver evidence-based, culturally relevant clinical prevention interventions and strategies" (AACN, 2011, p. 25) before entering the scholarly conversation to advise their peers.

The master's graduate will participate in the discourse of scholars as a practitioner, an educator, and a preceptor while providing opportunities for others to join the conversation. They will attend professional conferences to participate in scholarly conversation and contribute to the literature of the profession with original research, seeing gaps in the literature as opportunities for further scholarship.

4.3.4 The Essentials of Doctoral Education for Advanced Nursing Practice

Advanced Practice Nurses (APN) apply a broad spectrum of information to their practice decisions; therefore they consult other practitioners; consider diverse, evidence-based interventions; and apply their experience and clinical judgment before making a determination.

The AACN Essentials (AACN, 2006) focus much of the APN use of information to influence public policy, community health, and practice issues. They attend to the conversation of the scholars to analyze scientific data for the benefit of individual, corporate, and population health. Research may involve analysis of health policies and policy proposals; care delivery models related to environmental or occupational health; cultural and social dimensions of health; and outcomes of practice within a practice setting, institution, or health care organization.

"The integration of knowledge from diverse sources and across disciplines, and the application of knowledge to solve practice problems and improve health outcomes are only two of the many ways new phenomena and knowledge are generated other than through research" (AACN, 2006, p. 11).

To move the scholarly conversation forward nurses contribute on a national level through publishing, presentations at conferences as well as facilitating professional discussions based on their research and synthesis of information gleaned from divergent sources.

4.4 THE RESEARCH-FOCUSED DOCTORAL PROGRAM IN NURSING: PATHWAYS TO EXCELLENCE

The researched-focused doctoral nurse is expected to master in-depth knowledge in an essential area of the nursing field; understand the evolving roles and responsibilities of a nurse scholar; lead in advancing the profession; contribute to the global community of scholars; and take a position of leadership related to health policy and professional issues. Scholarship, according to Pathways to Excellence (AACN, 2010), includes "research, teaching, mentoring and service to the profession" (AACN, 2010, p. 5). The doctoral nurse takes part in research experiences, integrating different science perspectives and participates in interdisciplinary research teams.

They have a strong commitment to a research career which demands a sustained interest in research and scholarly communication. They display a pattern of scholarly writing on their own or in collaboration with other scholars which results in peer-reviewed publications and presentations of scholarly work. The PhD prepared nurse, more than any other, is committed to the conversation of scholars: gathering information from peers; answering the questions of the profession through conducting original research; offering their knowledge to the community of scholars; advancing nursing practice through creating useful evidence; and mentoring fellow nurses.

4.5 CONCLUSION

The never-ending conversation of nursing scholars includes nurses from the prelicensed nurse through the doctoral levels of practice and research. Nurses depend on the scholarly conversation to provide the best care possible; therefore they engage in acquiring information from appropriate sources assessing the quality of the source and the validity of the information they find; synthesizing the information from a variety of disciplines; consulting experts and peers in the nursing community; and conducting original research before determining how to move forward in patient care or practice decisions.

APPENDIX 4.1. TEACHING TIPS

Nurse educators and nursing librarians can facilitate nursing students learning by using any of the following teaching tips:

- Create individualized care plans based on patient values, clinical expertise, and evidence.
- Identify, collect, and mine raw data from researchers in multiple disciplines to apply to nursing practice.
- Integrate knowledge from diverse sources and across disciplines and then apply this knowledge to solve practice problems and improve health outcomes.
- Translate current evidence into practice and evaluate the outcomes.
- Question rationale for routine approaches to care that result in less-than-desired outcomes or adverse events.
- Evaluate personal facility for EBP by taking the Readiness for Evidence-Based Practice Survey, from the article: Provikoff, Tanner & Pierce (2005). CE Credit: Readiness of U.S. nurses for evidence-based practice. AJN, 105 (9): 40–52.
- Update teaching, training, and patient education materials.
- Update clinical knowledge including protocols, procedures, care plans, practice guidelines, complementary and alternative medicine, and pharmaceutical approaches.
- Present information in different formats for different audiences/ purposes (e.g., care plan, patient instruction, practice guideline, poster, podium presentation, blog post, scholarly article, etc.).
- Discuss and provide examples of different research designs for a variety of purposes.
- Write a research journal or some other record of the processes used over time to find, evaluate, and communicate health information. Revisit this record and identify opportunities for growth and learning.
- Discuss the concept of translational research and the ways in which it can contribute to patient care over time. Describe ways in which a specific biomedical research finding could be applied to patient care, clinical practice, and/or community health.
- Use a visual representation of the Information Cycle in the health sciences to initiate a discussion of how students might contribute as researchers, practitioners, educators, and authors.
- Use examples to demonstrate correct citation of references and practices reading citations from a variety of sources. Discuss the historical development of citation styles, and how they demonstrate the values of the discipline they represent (Health Sciences Interest Group, 2013).

REFERENCES

American Association of Colleges of Nursing. (2006). *The essentials of doctoral education for advanced nursing practice.* Retrieved from http://www.aacn.nche.edu/dnp/Essentials.pdf-Accessed September 5, 2017.

American Association of Colleges of Nursing. (2008). *The essentials of baccalaureate education for professional nursing practice.* Retrieved from http://www.aacn.nche.edu/education-resources/BaccEssentials08.pdf.

American Association of Colleges of Nursing. (2010). *The research-focused doctoral program in nursing: Pathways to excellence.* Retrieved from http://www.aacn.nche.edu/education-resources/PhDPosition.pdf.

American Association of Colleges of Nursing. (2011). *The essentials of master's education in nursing.* Retrieved from http://www.aacn.nche.edu/education-resources/MastersEssentials11.pdf.

American Nurses Association. (2015). *Incivility, bullying, and workplace violence.* Retrieved from http://www.nursingworld.org/MainMenuCategories/WorkplaceSafety/Healthy-Nurse/bullyingworkplaceviolence/Incivility-Bullying-and-Workplace-Violence.html.

Association of College & Research Libraries. (2013). *The information literacy competency standards for nursing.* Retrieved from http://www.ala.org/acrl/standards/nursing.

Association of College & Research Libraries. (2016). *Framework for information literacy for higher education.* Retrieved from http://www.ala.org/acrl/sites/ala.org.acrl/files/content/issues/infolit/Framework_ILHE.pdf.

Brown, D., & McCormack, B. (2016). Exploring psychological safety as a component of facilitation within the Promoting Action on Research Implementation in Health Services framework. *Journal of Clinical Nursing, 25,* 2921–2932. https://doi.org/10.1111/jocn.13348.

Burke, K. (1941). *The philosophy of literary form: Studies in symbolic action.* Baton Rouge: Louisiana State University Press.

Cantelon, P. L. (2010). NINR: Bringing science to life. National Institute of Nursing Research. Retrieved from: https://permanent.access.gpo.gov/gpo32758/NINR_History_Book_508.pdf (Accessed 5 January 2017). Accessed 05.03.17.

Cronenwett, L., Sherwood, G., Barnsteiner, J., Disch, J., Johnson, J., Mitchell, P., et al. (2007). Quality and safety education for nurses. *Nursing Outlook, 55*(3), 122–131.

Fulton, J. S. (2015). Engaging in scholarly conversation. Editorial *Clinical Nurse Specialist, 29*(1), 5. https://doi.org/10.1097/01.NUR.0000458911.71558.be.

Health Sciences Interest Group. (2013). *Teaching tips—Mapping to the ACRL information literacy competency standards for nursing.* Retrieved from https://healthsciencesinterestgroup.wikispaces.com/Teaching+Tips+-+Mapping+to+the+ACRL+Information+Literacy+Competency+Standards+for+Nursing.

Limoges, J., & Acorn, S. (2016). Transforming practice into clinical scholarship. *Journal of Advanced Nursing, 72*(4), 747–753.

Limoges, J., Acorn, S., & Osborne, M. (2015). The scholarship of application: Recognizing and promoting nurses' contribution to knowledge development. *The Journal of Continuing Education in Nursing, 46*(2), 77–82. https://doi.org/10.3928/00220124–20151217-02.

Myers, G., Cote-Arsenault, D., Worral, P., Rolland, R., Deppoliti, D., Duxbury, E., et al. (2016). A cross-hospital exploration of nurses' experiences with horizontal violence. *Journal of Nursing Management, 24,* 624–633. https://doi.org/10.1111/jonm.12365.

National Institute of Nursing Research. (2016). Mission Statement. https://www.ninr.nih.gov/aboutninr/ninr-mission-and-strategic-plan (Accessed 11 January 2016).

Nay, R. (2003). Evidence-based practice: Does it benefit older people and gerontic nursing? *Geriatric Nursing, 24*(6), 338–342.

Supporting Clinical Care. (2016). An institute in evidence-based practice for medical librarians. Aurora, Colorado: Health Sciences Library University of Colorado Anschutz Medical Campus, July 14–17, 2016.

Tafuria, S., Gallonea, M. S., Cappellia, M. G., Martinelli, D., Prato, R., & Germinario, C. (2014). Addressing the anti-vaccination movement and the role of HCWs. *Vaccine*, *32*(8), https://doi.org/10.1016/j.vaccine.2013.11.006.

FURTHER READING

Dollaghan, C. (2007). *The handbook for evidence-based practice in communication disorders.* Baltimore: Paul H. Brookes Pub.

National Institute of Nursing Research. (2016). *NINR strategic plan: Advancing science, improving lives.* Retrieved from https://www.ninr.nih.gov/aboutninr/ninr-mission-and-strategic-plan.

Nightingale, F. (1969). *Notes on nursing: What it is and what it is not.* New York: Dover Publications.

University of Maryland School of Nursing: Living History Museum. (n.d.). History of the School of Nursing. Retrieved from https://www.nursing.umaryland.edu/about/community/museum/virtual-tour/foundation/ Accessed 05.03.17.

CHAPTER 5

The Research Process

Kathryn Vela
Washington State University, Spokane, WA, United States

When Sackett and Rosenberg (1995) first introduced the concept of evidence-based practice, he described a five-step process: ask the clinical question, search for evidence, appraise the evidence, integrate the evidence, and evaluate the outcome. Melnyk, Fineout-Overholt, Stillwell, and Williamson (2010) added a "Step Zero," which is to "cultivate a spirit of inquiry" (p. 1). This ongoing curiosity is what drives nurses to ask critical questions of established procedures that can lead to beneficial practice-changing research.

5.1 FRAMEWORK FOR INFORMATION LITERACY FOR HIGHER EDUCATION

The ACRL Framework (2016) describes the sense of curiosity that underlies the research process under the concept "Research as Inquiry," saying "research is iterative and depends upon asking increasingly complex or new questions whose answers in turn develop additional questions or lines of inquiry in any field," (p. 7). Research is an evolving and never-ending process that focuses on filling the gaps in the current body of knowledge. Nurses who engage in research must be prepared to maintain an open mind and be willing to adjust their search strategy to fit the information they discover. Inquiry exists on a spectrum, which ranges from simple questions that allow novice learners to acquire strategic perspectives and a greater repertoire of investigative methods, to the complex questions that use more advanced research methods and explore diverse disciplinary perspectives. Experts in research will recognize the collaborative effort involved in expanding the collective knowledge of their field and engage in dialogues that work to deepen the conversation around the research.

The Frame emphasizes that the results of research often have implications for patient care, and the process of inquiry may focus upon personal, professional, or societal needs. For example, research in the area of aging and aging health policy will be critical to providing care to an increasing number of elderly patients in the near future (Ortman, Velkoff, & Hogan, 2014).

Nurses can pursue lines of research that affect the established protocols and standards of care in their field. In doing so, they provide new evidence that can "improve nursing practice, nursing education, or the delivery of nursing services," (National League for Nursing, 2010).

The knowledge practices of this frame describe the progression of skills learned when engaging with the research process. At the most basic level, nursing students and professionals need to formulate questions based on gaps or conflicts in the research and to determine the most appropriate methods of investigation. To properly limit the scope of investigation, learners must be able to simplify complex questions by breaking them into their component concepts using frameworks such as PICO. The PICO frameworks allow researchers to separate a query into unique concepts to search for individually: patient/population, intervention, comparison, and outcome. They should know several different research methods and be able to employ them based on need, circumstance, and type of inquiry. The expert researcher will know that research and evidence-based practice is an iterative process that builds new knowledge as it creates more questions. As such, researchers should be able to monitor and organize information in a way that allows them to "draw reasonable conclusions based on the analysis and interpretation of information" (ACRL, 2016, p. 7).

Much of nursing research is quantitative in nature, but nursing students and professionals must include qualitative research, particularly for research questions asking how or why a phenomenon occurs. In some instances, qualitative research is a precursor to further quantitative inquiry, which can then be generalized into a conclusion or conclusions that can apply to an entire population. In other cases, qualitative research can stand on its own as conclusions are applied to individuals in similar contexts as the research study (Miller, 2010). There is also a third possibility that of a mixed methods study that combines qualitative and quantitative methods to create a more comprehensive assessment of the research query. The expert researcher will know that both quantitative and qualitative research has value in the field of nursing and will be able to apply the information gathered from both types of inquiry to the question at hand.

However, researchers should also know that the results of inquiry can be inconclusive or raise additional questions. It is not uncommon to see a call for more research on a topic at the end of the published study. Inconclusive results can be caused by errors in research design such as inappropriate methodology or incorrect analysis, or they can indicate the need for a new hypothesis. In either case, the inconclusive results have value in terms of the general body of nursing knowledge and should be acknowledged. Researchers in nursing need to be aware of different types of bias that can result from inconclusive or negative results: studies that are never published due to their undesirable outcomes cause study publication bias, while studies that publish only the positive or statistically significant results lead to outcome reporting bias (Howland, 2011). With this in mind, the expert researcher will be able to critically view results and methodologies in order to determine their validity and relevance to their inquiry.

As students and nurses are developing their research abilities, they should seek to cultivate attitudes toward research that support iterative, engaged, and open-minded inquiry. Learners should be aware that simple questions may still be important to the growth of their field and should use those inquires to develop new investigative methods. Higher-level researchers will come to value "persistence, adaptability, and flexibility and recognize that ambiguity can benefit the research process." Researchers at all levels ask themselves what they know and how they know it and will seek multiple perspectives throughout the research process.

5.2 INFORMATION LITERACY COMPETENCY STANDARDS FOR NURSING (ILCSN)

Standard One of the ILSCN states, "The information literate nurse determines the nature and extent of the information needed," (2013). Standard Three builds on this, saying "the information literate nurse critically evaluates the procured information and its sources, and as a result, decides whether or not to modify the initial query and/or seek additional sources and whether to develop a new research process," (ACRL, 2013). Together, the performance indicators and outcomes of the first and third standards describe the research process with emphasis on the necessary underlying spirit of inquiry that drives innovation.

The nurse, when identifying a research topic, thinks about the "links, patterns, and inconsistencies between the topic, current practice and broader health context," (Royal College of Nursing [RCN], 2011, p. 5). With a topic in mind, they can form a focused question by breaking it down into unique concepts with a PICO framework, (as described in Table 5.1), and having done so, develop a hypothesis or thesis statement and devises questions based on the information need. If a nurse is exploring the impact of vaccines on the elderly population, they may ask "for patients 65 years and older (P), how does the use of an influenza vaccine (I) influence the risk

Table 5.1 A description of the PICO framework and its variations

Clinical query components	Description	Example
P—Patient or population	The most important characteristic of the patient or group	Age Gender Ethnicity
I—Intervention	The treatment or diagnostic test	Drug Surgery Policy
C—Comparison (optional)	The alternative under consideration	No treatment Current practice
O—Outcome	The desired state of the patient or group as a result of the intervention	Lower blood pressure Quicker recovery
T—Time OR Type of question	The amount of time for the intervention or data collection OR The category of the query	6 months OR Therapy
T—Type of Study Design	The format of the desired evidence	Randomized controlled trial

of developing pneumonia (O) during the flu season?" (the [C] component would be "no influenza vaccine"). With the research question in mind, the nurse selects potential sources from various disciplines and in various formats that provide information from background knowledge to foreground research.

The nurse will cultivate a working knowledge of literature in nursing-related fields, including how information is produced, organized, and disseminated as well as the ability to recognize primary and secondary sources. In doing so, they will be able to retrieve the correct types of information that best support their research query. For example, a textbook may provide an overview of the topic while a journal article contains currency and detail (RCN, 2011). They will know to consider the influence of how knowledge is organized into disciplines and combinations of disciplines and to value archival information and the preservation of information in general. The nurse will need to consider the costs and benefits of acquiring the needed information, by determining the availability and adjusting the information seeking process beyond locally held resources. To this end, they will be aware and take advantage of the information retrieval resources and experts at their disposal; for instance, if their hospital or institution has a library, they may contact the librarian to use the interlibrary loan service to retrieve articles and sources.

Throughout the research process, the nurse will know that research is an iterative process and will evaluate and refine the original PICO question in response to new information. They will be able to identify gaps in the literature, which can inform additional avenues of inquiry. A common opportunity for this lies in the "future research" sections of most studies, where the authors describe how their research question can be further explored. To make information choices, the nurse will describe and make use of criteria that guide the research process. As the nurse seeks to identify information needs, they will question assumptions and seek new insights that will drive the body of nursing research forward.

The nurse is able to identify and summarize main ideas from gathered sources and apply them to the appropriate element of the research question. As they do so, the nurse is able to evaluate the information and its sources for reliability, validity, accuracy, authority, currency, and bias. The reputation of a journal, the geographic origin of the data, and the type of study are examples of factors that can influence these variables (RCN, 2011). Once they have verified the relevance and quality of the information, the nurse synthesizes the main ideas to answer the research question and when possible, extends these conclusions to a higher level in order to create new questions and hypotheses.

It is worth noting the existence of a nursing culture that is somewhat resistant to long-term and sustainable change. It has historically been challenging to narrow the research-to-practice gap, and innovation in the field of nursing typically does not last long term (Fleiszer, 2016). Watkins, Dewar, and Kennedy (2016) suggest appreciative inquiry as a methodology that would support investigation, development, and change in nursing practice by using existing strengths in practice to serve as a launching point for improvement and sustainability. The nurse will seek to use methodologies such as this to facilitate long-term positive change in their practice environment.

With new research information at hand and an understanding of the need for continuous improvement, the nurse compares this knowledge with prior knowledge to determine whether the information contradicts or verifies current practice. They are able to integrate new information with their existing body of knowledge and are careful to maintain a neutral position, including information that may contradict their value system. The Royal College of Nursing reminds nurses to "acknowledge contradictions between values expressed in the information and own values,"

(Royal College of Nursing, 2011, p. 9). As such, the nurse participates in discussions of the information to validate understanding and improve interpretation, with interprofessional teams, professional association discussion lists, networks, and at professional conferences.

5.3 PROGRESSION OF NURSING EDUCATION AND PRACTICE

5.3.1 The Quality and Safety Education for Nurses (QSEN)—Prelicensure

From the beginning of their education, nurses are required to demonstrate the knowledge, skills, and attitudes (KSAs) regarding the value and appraisal of information. The QSEN describes the need for nurses to be able to engage in evidence-based practice by "[differentiating] clinical opinion from research and evidence summaries" (Cronenwett et al., 2007, p. 5). This stimulates the process of inquiry as the nurse seeks to locate original research and evidence reports related to the area of practice, ideally in relevant professional journals. In doing so, the prelicensure nurse develops an appreciation for staying current in their field and creates a habit of critically evaluating evidence that could stimulate further research.

As they learn to locate and evaluate evidence for inquiry, the QSEN requires that the prelicensure nurse will be able to "explain the role of evidence in determining best clinical practice" (Cronenwett et al., 2007, p. 5). They will develop the skill set to be able to "challenge the status quo, question underlying assumptions, and offer new insights to improve the quality of care for patients," (National League for Nursing, 2010). In this way, the prelicensure nurse will recognize the need for continuous improvement in clinical practice, and that positive change is based on new and discovered knowledge integrated with clinical expertise.

5.3.2 The Essentials of Baccalaureate Education for Professional Nursing Practice

Professional nursing practice is grounded in the translation of current evidence into practice. Nurses must use skills of inquiry, analysis, and information literacy to address practice issues (AACN, 2008). Scholarship for the baccalaureate graduate involves the identification of information needs; appraisal and integration of evidence; and evaluation of outcomes (AACN, 2008). In doing so, they demonstrate an understanding of the basic elements of the research process and models for applying evidence to clinical practice (AACN, 2008).

Baccalaureate graduates must be able to evaluate data from all relevant sources, including technology, to inform the delivery of care (AACN, 2008). In order to properly evaluate and critique information sources, nurses should consider the levels of evidence: textbooks, case studies, reviews of literature, research critiques, controlled trials, evidence-based clinical practice guidelines, meta-analyses, and systematic reviews (e.g., www.guideline. gov and the Cochrane Database of Systematic Reviews) (AACN, 2008). In knowing whether the information contained in the sources is background or foreground research, nurses can appropriately apply the information to the research process.

As stated in The Essentials of Baccalaureate Education for Professional Nursing Practice, "baccalaureate nurses integrate reliable evidence from multiple ways of knowing to inform practice and make clinical judgments" (AACN, 2008, p. 17). During their education, emphasis should be placed on integrating the knowledge and methods of a variety of disciplines to support decision-making in practice (AACN, 2008). Nurses must be able to incorporate evidence, clinical judgment, interprofessional perspectives, and patient preferences in planning, implementing, and evaluating outcomes of care (AACN, 2008). They should also be able to make use of technology and information systems for clinical decision-making (AACN, 2008).

Learning does not stop once a nurse earns a baccalaureate degree. Knowledge is increasingly complex and evolving rapidly. Therefore, baccalaureate graduates are expected to focus on continuous self-evaluation and lifelong learning as a way to better understand themselves and others, and to contribute to safe, quality care (AACN, 2008). There are many opportunities for continuing education, both at the national level with the American Nurses Association and at the state level with state nursing associations. Nurses can also pursue higher degree levels in order to expand the depth of their knowledge of nursing practice and research.

5.3.3 The Essentials of Masters Education in Nursing

A master's education in nursing builds on baccalaureate knowledge and experience to equip a nurse with the skills necessary to engage in a higher level of practice and research. Graduates of a master's program will be prepared to translate current evidence into practice and apply an inquiring attitude toward their practice and care environment (AACN, 2011). They will be able to gather, document, and analyze outcome data that serve as a foundation for decision-making and the implementation of interventions or strategies to improve care outcomes. The masters graduate nurse uses statistical and epidemiological principles to synthesize these data, information, and knowledge to evaluate and achieve optimal health outcomes (AACN, 2011).

The masters graduate nurse can engage in a process of identifying relevant questions by finding problems and gaps in evidence for clinical practice (AACN, 2011). When gathering information, nurses can distinguish between primary and secondary sources and decide when each type of information is relevant to the question. For example, they can determine when a qualitative approach such as grounded theory is more appropriate than a randomized controlled trial. Nurses can evaluate the outcomes of research and identify additional questions that arise as a result of their analysis (AACN, 2011). With their high-level understanding of evidence-based practice, nurses are prepared to "lead continuous improvement processes based on translational research skills" and "apply research outcomes within the practice setting" (AACN, 2011, p. 16).

Nurses serve as information managers, patient advocates, and educators by assisting others (including patients, students, caregivers, and healthcare professionals) in accessing, understanding, evaluating, and applying health-related information (AACN, 2011). They "support staff in lifelong learning to improve care decisions" by acting as an example for evidence-based decision-making (AACN, 2011, p. 16). The masters graduate nurse provides guidance for health education programs, evidence-based policies, and point-of-care practices that support the application and understanding of research outcomes to clinical practice.

5.3.4 The Essentials of Doctoral Education for Advanced Nursing Practice

Doctoral programs in nursing are designed to prepare nurses to be scholars and scientists, with curriculum emphasis on scientific content and research methodology (AACN, 2006). DNP graduates are able to translate research into practice as they disseminate and integrate new knowledge in their field (AACN, 2006). In addition to analyzing and participating in research, nurses know to incorporate knowledge from diverse sources and across disciplines with an open mind to improve practice and health outcomes (AACN, 2006).

The DNP program prepares nurses to use information technology and research methods to perform several key components of the research process (AACN, 2006). They are able use these tools to collect data to generate evidence that can be applied to nursing practice, and they can inform the design of databases that generate useful and relevant evidence (AACN, 2006). DNP graduates will be able to design evidence-based interventions that will result in valid and meaningful results and know how to identify gaps in evidence that are relevant to practice (AACN, 2006).

Nurses in DNP programs will have the skills to "develop and evaluate care delivery approaches that meet current and future needs of patient populations based on scientific findings in nursing and other clinical sciences" (AACN, 2006, p. 10). They will be able to synthesize literature and research-based knowledge to find and implement the best evidence for practice (AACN, 2006). The result of these efforts will be improved healthcare outcomes as practice continuously evolves to meet patient needs.

5.4 THE RESEARCH-FOCUSED DOCTORAL PROGRAM IN NURSING: PATHWAYS TO EXCELLENCE

A research-focused doctoral program in nursing will prepare graduates to develop and communicate the knowledge of the field to lay and professional audiences. PhD graduates will also be able to identify implications for policy, nursing practice, and the lay profession. Curricular emphasis will be on mastering scientific methods, including team science, as well as developing skills for advanced research design and statistical methods. Graduates of this program will also be able to prepare research grants and manuscripts for publication (AACN, 2010).

Nurses in research-focused DNP programs will be expected to integrate the concepts of scholarship throughout their career, including research, teaching, mentoring, and service to the profession. They will be well prepared to assume leadership roles in the field to engage and support knowledge that informs nursing science and to influence evidence-based health policy (AACN, 2010). Being well-acquainted with the importance of research and its applications to practice, graduates of research-focused DNP programs will work to actively improve the rigor of nursing inquiry and promote critical evaluation of evidence as it impacts health outcomes.

5.5 CONCLUSION

The importance of research to the continued progression of nursing knowledge cannot be understated. Throughout the education of a nurse, they must be encouraged to "raise questions, challenge traditional and existing practices, and seek creative approaches to problems," (National League for Nursing). The development of this spirit of inquiry begins by finding and evaluating evidence in the literature and processes to identifying gaps and formulating research questions. As their understanding of the research process becomes more advanced, nurses will be able to collect, analyze, and integrate new data that addresses disparities in evidence and evaluate the impact of new evidence-based approaches on patient outcomes. Throughout their education and career, nurses will harness their curiosity to drive research and improvement for the benefit of their patients and communities.

APPENDIX 5.1. TEACHING TIPS

Nurse educators and nursing librarians can facilitate nursing students learning by using any of the following teaching tips (Health Sciences Interest Group, 2013):

- Compose a PICO(TT) question from a sample topic.
- List synonyms that could be used for searching a given PICO(TT) question. Compare results of searches using different keywords.
- Appraise search results for relevance to the PICO(TT) question used. Evaluate the best way to search for this particular question.
- Summarize current evidence regarding major diagnostic and treatment actions within the practice specialty.
- Take the Plagiarism Self Test as homework such as the one from Western Carolina University's Writing Center.
- Summarize the main ideas of an article addresses a research question, using PICO(TT) format if appropriate.

Identify an article from a discipline other than medicine or nursing that is relevant to their research question after searching a multidisciplinary database such as Academic Search Complete.

REFERENCES

American Association of Colleges of Nursing. (2006). *The essentials of doctoral educaton for advanced nursing practice.* Retrieved from http://www.aacn.nche.edu/dnp/Essentials.pdf-Accessed September 4, 2017.

American Association of Colleges of Nursing. (2008). *The essentials of baccalaureate education for professional nursing practice.* Retrieved from http://www.aacn.nche.edu/education-resources/BaccEssentials08.pdf.

American Association of Colleges of Nursing. (2010). *The research-focused doctoral program in nursing: Pathways to excellence.* Retrieved from http://www.aacn.nche.edu/education-resources/PhDPosition.pdf.

American Association of Colleges of Nursing. (2011). *The essentials of master's education in nursing.* Retrieved from http://www.aacn.nche.edu/education-resources/MastersEssentials11.pdf.

Association of College & Research Libraries. (2013). *The information literacy competency standards for nursing.* Retrieved from http://www.ala.org/acrl/standards/nursing.

Association of College & Research Libraries. (2016). *Framework for information literacy for higher education.* Retrieved from http://www.ala.org/acrl/sites/ala.org.acrl/files/content/issues/infolit/Framework_ILHE.pdf.

Cronenwett, L., Sherwood, G., Barnsteiner, J., Disch, J., Johnson, J., Mitchell, P., et al. (2007). Quality and safety education for nurses. *Nursing Outlook, 55*(3), 122–131.

Fleiszer, A. R. (2016). A unit-level perspective on the long-term sustainability of a nursing best practice guidelines program: An embedded multiple case study. *International Journal of Nursing Studies, 53*, 204–218. https://doi.org/10.1016/j.ijnurstu.2015.09.004.

Health Sciences Interest Group. (2013). *Teaching tips—Mapping to the ACRL information literacy competency standards for nursing.* Retrieved from https://healthscienceinterestgroup.wikispaces.com/Teaching+Tips+-+Mapping+to+the+ACRL+Information+Literacy+Competency+Standards+for+Nursing.

Howland, R. H. (2011). What you see depends on where you're looking and how you look at it. *Journal of Psychosocial Nursing, 49*(8).

Melnyk, B. M., Fineout-Overholt, E., Stillwell, S. B., & Williamson, K. M. (2010). Evidence-based practice: Step-by-step: The seven steps of evidence-based practice. *American Journal of Nursing, 110*(1), 51–53. https://doi.org/10.1097/01.NAJ.0000366056.06605.d2.

Miller, W. R. (2010). Qualitative research findings as evidence: Utility in nursing practice. *Clinical Nurse Specialist, 24*(4), 191–193. https://doi.org/10.1097/NUR.0b013e3181e36087.

National League for Nursing. (2010). *Outcomes and competencies for graduates of practical/vocational, diploma, associate degree, baccalaureate, master's, practice doctorate, and research doctorate programs in nursing.* New York, NY: National League for Nursing.

Ortman, J. M., Velkoff, V. A., & Hogan, H. (2014). *An aging nation: The older population of the United States.* United States Census Bureau, Populations and Projections, Current Population Reports. Retrieved from https://www.census.gov/prod/2014pubs/p25-1140.pdf.

Royal College of Nursing. (2011). *RCN competencies: Finding, using and managing information: Nursing, midwifery, health and social care information literacy competencies.* Retrieved from https://www2.rcn.org.uk/__data/assets/pdf_file/0005/276449/003053.pdf.

Sackett, D. L., & Rosenberg, W. M. (1995). The need for evidence-based medicine. *Journal of the Royal Society of Medicine, 88*(11), 620–624.

Watkins, S., Dewar, B., & Kennedy, C. (2016). Appreciative inquiry as an intervention to change nursing practice in in-patient settings: An integrative review. *International Journal of Nursing Studies, 60*, 179–190. https://doi.org/10.1016/j.ijnurstu.2016.04.017.

CHAPTER 6

Finding Relevant Information

Kathryn Vela
Washington State University, Spokane, WA, United States

In order for nurses to be able to conduct quality and beneficial research, they must possess the searching skills necessary to locate the relevant evidence in the literature. Given the increasingly high volume of medical research in existence, the ability to design an appropriate query and a successful search strategy are more important to clinical nursing practice than ever before. Evidence-based practice requires that nurses develop a "systematic approach to searching multiple databases to ensure that the resulting evidence is relevant" to the information need (Melnyk et al., 2017). Such a skillset will allow nurses to harness their curiosity and contribute to the growing body of nursing knowledge.

6.1 FRAMEWORK FOR INFORMATION LITERACY FOR HIGHER EDUCATION

The ACRL Framework (2016) describes "Searching as Strategic Exploration," furthermore "searching for information is often nonlinear and iterative, requiring the evaluation of a range of information sources and the mental flexibility to pursue alternate avenues as new understanding develops" (p. 9). With a question in mind to guide the process, searching involves identifying both possible sources and determining how to access those sources. Nurses who are learning how to search effectively may use few search strategies to identify a limited number of sources. As they develop expertise, they can utilize a variety of search strategies based on the scope and context of the information need which will allow them to search more broadly and deeply. Expert searchers realize that the information seeking process is a complex experience that both affects and is affected by the cognitive, affective, and social aspects of the searcher.

The knowledge practices of this frame describe the progression of skills learned when engaging with the searching process. Novice searchers need to develop the ability to determine the scope of the information-seeking task, which will allow them to accurately identify interested parties who

The Intersection. https://doi.org/10.1016/B978-0-08-101282-6.00006-2

might produce information on that topic. Once identified, they also need to establish how to access that information. Learners need to be able to utilize both divergent and convergent thinking as they search. They should know how to select appropriate search strategies and tools based on their information need and refine their strategies as necessary. The expert searcher will be able to augment their searching strategies and access relevant information by drawing on their understanding of how information systems are organized.

As students and nurses are developing their research abilities, they should seek to cultivate attitudes toward searching that support flexible, creative, and iterative research. Learners should be aware that, depending on the scope of the information need, sources vary in content and format and have varying relevance and value. They will understand that initial searching attempts do not always produce the desired results and will seek assistance from searching experts such as librarians. Higher-level searchers will recognize the value of browsing and other serendipitous methods of information gathering. Searchers of all levels will persevere in spite of search challenges and know when they have enough information to complete the task.

6.2 INFORMATION LITERACY COMPETENCY STANDARDS FOR NURSING (ILCSN)

Standard One of the ILCSN states "the information literate nurse determines the nature and extent of the information needed" (ACRL, 2013). Additionally, Standard Two asserts that "the information literate nurse accesses needed information effectively and efficiently" (ACRL, 2013). A third ILCSN standard, Standard Three, states "the information literate nurse critically evaluates the procured information and its sources, and as a result, decides whether or not to modify the initial query and/or seek additional sources and whether to develop a new research process" (ACRL, 2013). These standards encompass the practical skills necessary for a nurse to design and execute an effective search strategy. They must be able to define the information need at the beginning of the searching process and use these parameters to apply the most appropriate investigative methods to their query.

Constructing and implementing an efficient and effectivelydesigned search strategy requires a high level of expertise. The nurse will be able to create a strategic approach that addresses each element of the PICO question. The nurse identifies keywords, synonyms, and related terms based on the PICO question and combines them using the appropriate commands for the information retrieval system selected. They may also utilize subject searching by using the hierarchies of subject terms (e.g., MeSH and CINAHL), which will allow for more precise results. The expert searcher will be able to use these skills to create search strategies that locate nursing theories and philosophies as well as grey literature such as conference proceedings and theses. The amount of information discovered can be controlled with the use of Boolean operators or commands such as "and," "or," and "not" (Royal College of Nursing [RCN], 2011). They will be able to find additional relevant information by following citations and cited references within publications.

One thing to note about PICO is that there are different variations on the framework depending on the information need. The PICOT framework adds a time element to the construction of a research question, which describes either the length of time the treatment is prescribed or how long data is collected (Davies, 2011). The PICOTT framework refers to the type of question and the type of study design to answer the research query (Davies, 2011). The nurse will maintain a familiarity with each of these frameworks and be able to utilize the framework elements (as illustrated in Fig. 6.1) to design an effective research question.

The nurse will know not to directly translate PICO terms to search terms, as the results will be too specific to be useful. There is no hard and fast method to turning a PICO question into search terms and keywords; rather it is a flexible process that varies depending on the results found. However, there are some strategies that will help the nurse to locate relevant information based on a PICO question. Brainstorming words or phrases with similar meanings to those in the PICO question will expand the breadth of the search in a helpful way, as will expanding acronyms to their full form; for example, using both "ED" and "emergency department" as keywords. Searchers should also look at subject headings like MeSH terms and CINAHL headings to find the terms used by databases to categorize the information being sought. Advanced searchers will be able to view the hierarchy within the controlled vocabulary to explore other subject headings and give context to limiting terms.

Once an information need has been defined, the nurse can identify various types and formats of potential sources for information. This includes locating disciplines that produce information on the topic and publications where that information is published, being sure to include sources from throughout the progression from background to foreground research.

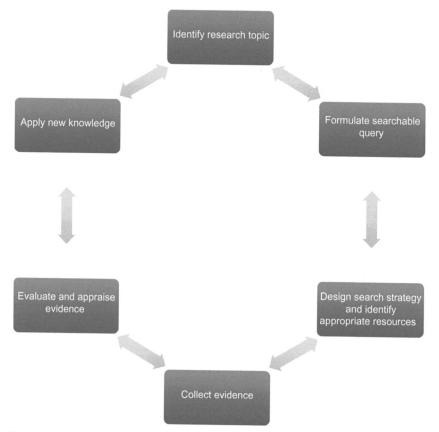

Fig. 6.1 The research process is an iterative one and will be repeated several times over the course of investigating a clinical topic.

Patient records, audit results, and clinical experts can also be sources although the nurse should take care to use such sources appropriately (RCN, 2011). They will have a strong understanding of how information is produced in nursing-related fields and will be able to recognize both primary and secondary sources of information in nursing. The nurse will know to include the literature of professional nursing associations and field-specific sources like manuals and handbook standards in their search.

Throughout the searching process, as keywords and potential sources of information are identified, the nurse will need to reevaluate the nature and extent of the information need. They will understand that searching is an iterative process that changes based on what is discovered in the gathered information. If the search results are too broad, the nurse will alter the search terms to increase specificity and add more limiters; conversely, if the results are too narrow, the nurse will make the search terms more general and reduce the use of limiters. The nurse will refine the original information need in relation to what they have found by altering the PICO to build on what has already been discovered in the area of interest.

In addition to being able to find relevant information using appropriate search strategies, the nurse must also be able to retrieve information using a variety of methods. They know to search more than one, two, or even three databases in order to achieve the greatest coverage of available knowledge. For example, PubMed and CINAHL are obvious database choices, but PsycINFO, Web of Science, and the Joanna Briggs Institute Library can be relevant sources as well. Searchers must be able to navigate information retrieval systems to access full-text articles, including links, link resolvers, and use of interlibrary loan. The advanced searcher will be comfortable utilizing information experts like librarians and library staff to navigate various classification schemes and other systems within the library and library catalog.

In the process of locating and accessing information, the nurse may find it necessary to refine the search strategy. Initially, this will involve using limiters such as date and population to refine the search results to more closely match what is being asked in the guiding PICO question. It can also involve limiting by publication type to identify and locate appropriate levels of evidence. As they develop searching expertise, nurses will employ "pearl growing," a searching technique where they select applicable subject headings from the records of relevant articles to refine search statements (Ramer, 2005). As the search progresses and is altered, the nurse will assess the quantity, quality, accuracy, currency, and relevance of the results and the search strategy to determine whether alternatives should be pursued. They identify gaps in the retrieved information and revise the search strategy to fill those gaps if necessary. Additional searches are performed using revised strategy or new systems or methods until the nurse decides that enough relevant information has been gathered (ACRL, 2013).

One of the often-overlooked steps in the searching process is the thoughtful management of the retrieved information. The nurse will maintain a record of the process in a journal or log for later reference, including keywords, subject headings, search history, information retrieval systems, and methods. They will select the most appropriate technology to copy, scan, and export information to citation management tools as necessary. A system for organizing the information using file management concepts will be in place, with standards for consistent file name, file format, and secure storage. The nurse will be able to understand the elements and syntax of multiple citation formats, and be able to identify the format recognized by the organization that they are writing for, whether that is a publisher, university, or employer (RCN, 2011). They will be care to ensure that each information source is properly cited with all pertinent information.

Once the relevant information has been located and properly stored, the nurse must be able to assess the strength of the evidence before they can begin to make practice recommendations. As Jones (2010) states, "[the] strength of the evidence is determined by synthesizing the information on level and quality of evidence supporting each practice recommendation," (p. 308). The level of evidence is based on the type of study design, i.e., systematic review, randomized controlled trial, etc. (Jones, 2010). The quality of evidence is determined based on such characteristics as consistency of results, sufficiency of sample size, level of control, and decisiveness of conclusions (Costa & Poe, 2012). Synthesizing evidence is a challenging and time-consuming task, but it is necessary for the nurse to be able to confidently recommend changes to current practice.

In addition to assessing and synthesizing the evidence, the advanced searcher will ensure that they take the time to evaluate the entire searching process, to determine possible improvements for future projects. This reflection will take place once the searching process has reached its final conclusion and the information need has been met. In determining what parts of the process were successful and what parts were not, the nurse can improve the efficiency and effectiveness of future searches for information. The nurse will always be prepared to incorporate new strategies and new information retrieval sources into their search process, as part of their dedication to life-long learning.

6.3 PROGRESSION OF NURSING EDUCATION AND PRACTICE

6.3.1 The Quality and Safety Education for Nurses (QSEN) Prelicensure

The QSEN for prelicensure nurses outlines basic knowledge, skills, and attitudes that they must possess in relation to finding relevant information. The QSEN standard for evidence-based practice states that the prelicensure nurse must "integrate best current evidence with clinical expertise and patient/family preferences and values" (Cronenwett et al., 2007). They must recognize the relationship between information management and safe patient care and be able to use electronic sources to locate quality healthcare information (Cronenwett et al., 2007). This will instill an appreciation of their own role in the "design, selection, implementation, and evaluation of information technologies to support patient care" (Cronenwett et al., 2007).

Their practical skills in using electronic information resources will support their ability to "locate evidence reports related to clinical practice topics and guidelines" (Cronenwett et al., 2007). This will allow the prelicensure nurse to differentiate between levels of evidence and describe their reliable sources to their healthcare team (Cronenwett et al., 2007). Implicit in this competency is the ability to formulate a search query to locate the evidence reports and alter their search strategy as necessary in order to find the appropriate level of evidence.

6.3.2 The Essentials of Baccalaureate Education for Professional Nursing Practice

As baccalaureate graduates progress through their education and practice in clinical settings, they will continue to use and hone their searching skills to address practice issues. They must be able to "[locate] health and other relevant research literature and other sources of evidence" (AACN, 2008, p. 17) in order to analyze and discuss key information related to the improvement of patient outcomes. At the baccalaureate level, nurses should be able to demonstrate the ability to use technology and information systems for clinical decision making, with emphasis on performing online literature searches to find relevant health information

The evidence-based practice behind clinical decision-making begins with the location of evidence, and baccalaureate graduates must be able to engage in this process in collaboration with other members of the healthcare team (AACN, 2008). To that end, they should be familiar with a variety of methods for locating and evaluating health information from the literature and other sources at multiple levels of evidence. Nurses should also have the technical skills to employ electronic database search strategies for prevalent systems such as CINAHL and PubMed.

In addition to locating evidence, the baccalaureate graduate nurse should be able to ethically manage information in order to "communicate effectively; provide safe and effective patient care; and use research and clinical evidence to inform practice decisions" (AACN, 2008, p. 18). The nurse will be able to select the appropriate technology to store information and maintain security and privacy while adhering to regulatory requirements (AACN, 2008). The thoughtful management of information will enable the nurse to maximize their searching efforts for the benefit of their clinical practice.

6.3.3 The Essentials of Master's Education in Nursing

At the master's level, nurses need to cultivate an inquiring attitude toward their practice and patient care environment. They should continually question and evaluate existing policies using current evidence and identifying gaps where such evidence is lacking. This requires the mastery of a variety of searching skills and strategies that will allow them to find the necessary information from reliable sources. If they are engaged in a leadership role, they may be required to support their staff in learning how to search for health information. They should be able to collaborate with their healthcare team to appropriately apply search techniques to information needs that will improve patient outcomes (AACN, 2011).

As the master's graduate nurse engages in continuous improvement processes, they will recognize that it mirrors the iterative process of searching for information. They must be able to lead their team in the cyclical process that includes "identifying questions needing answers, searching or creating the evidence for potential solutions/innovations, evaluating outcomes, and identifying additional questions" (AACN, 2011, p. 16). At their advanced level of searching, they will know to utilize information resources from multiple fields to develop a deeper understanding of the question at the "unit, clinic, home, [and] program level" (AACN, 2011, p. 9).

According to the American Nurses Association, the master's graduate nurse is expected to use current evidence to "expand knowledge, skills, abilities, and judgement; enhance role performance; and to increase knowledge of professional issues" (American Nurses Association, 2015). The searching skills that they have developed throughout their education will support this competency by enabling the nurse to effectively locate relevant clinical evidence from reliable sources. In addition, their leadership position within their healthcare team will allow the master's graduate nurse to encourage others to better develop their searching skills as well.

6.3.4 The Essentials of Doctoral Education for Advanced Nursing Practice

As they prepare to engage in scholarship and research, nurses in doctoral programs will learn how to "give meaning to isolated facts" and use "knowledge to solve a problem via the scholarship of application" (AACN, 2006a, p. 11). Even as they are involved in the process of creating new clinical evidence in the field of nursing, they must remain aware of what already exists on their topic of interest to ensure they are addressing a gap in practice. DNP graduate nurses do this by using information technology and research methods to collect data from reliable sources, thus facilitating the process of translating research into practice (AACN, 2006a).

The ability to design clinical recommendations from research evidence is a key skill expected of DNP graduate nurses. They must "outline systematic approaches to develop evidence-based clinical practice guidelines" to support planned organizational change (Stevens, 2005). Nurses at this level will be able to summarize their research evidence in terms of benefits, harms, and costs of different options (Stevens, 2005), which will allow other healthcare providers to make informed decisions based on the strength of the evidence along with patient preferences and clinical settings.

To successfully integrate new evidence into existing practice, the DNP graduate nurse must be able to make a strong case for the proposed change. It is crucial that they develop an understanding of the local factors and effective communication pathways in order to build partnerships, share information, provide training, and standardize the new practice (Dunning et al., 1998; International Council of Nurses, 2012). With the appropriate preparation and support, the DNP graduate nurse can "apply relevant findings to develop practice guidelines and improve practice and the practice environment" (AACN, 2006a, p. 12).

6.3.5 The research-focused doctoral program in nursing: Pathways to excellence

The research-focused doctoral program in nursing requires both "mastering and extending the knowledge of the discipline through research" (AACN, 2010, p. 4). The resources and infrastructure necessary for a PhD program require data, information, and knowledge management processing. The library and data knowledge base resources should be sufficient to support the scholarly endeavors of faculty and students and should provide access to online and print journals, books, literature, and search support; therefore, it follows that the PhD student would be expected to use them at a level beyond the Baccalaureate and Masters level students.

The PhD graduate is expected to conduct an independent program of research, seek necessary support, and include other clinicians and students in their work (AACN, 2006b). At this most advanced level, they must have the searching expertise to carry out a thorough review of the relevant literature in order to ensure that they are conducting research that will positively contribute to the existing body of nursing knowledge. In doing so, they will improve the scope and quality of research evidence that is used to create and revise clinical guidelines.

6.4 CONCLUSION

Throughout their education and careers, nurses will ask clinical questions that will require them to utilize skills and strategies to find information. The novice searcher will be able to use their question to design a diverse strategic approach to locating information that will address the identified practice gap. As they progress in skill and knowledge, they will assess the strength, quality, and level of the collected evidence, thus ensuring that they are analyzing only the most reliable and applicable information. Nurses at all levels will know to continuously reevaluate the search strategy and information need based on the collected results, and to be flexible in their search parameters and sources. Ultimately, the searching skills and strategies that nurses develop will support the integration of the best available clinical evidence into nursing practice and improve the patient experience.

APPENDIX 6.1. TEACHING TIPS

Nurse educators and nursing librarians can facilitate nursing students learning by using any of the following teaching tips (Health Sciences Interest Group, 2013):

- Watch the "PubMed for Nurses" video tutorials and complete the quizzes and exercises.
- Identify MeSH and CINAHL headings in a relevant database and compares search results from searching with subject terms vs. keywords.
- List of as many professional associations in their field as can be found in 5 min to Google search.
- Demonstrate ability to work through the iterative process of background research, databases for foreground research, and refining of PICO(TT) question after class demonstration.
- Search CINAHL and PubMed/MEDLINE to find an example of primary and secondary sources and quantitative and qualitative data on a sample topic.
- Demonstrate effective strategies for addressing a PICO(TT) question, identifying subject databases and search terms for each PICO(TT) element.
- Demonstrate a keyword search and a subject heading search on a specific topic. Identifies the results of each search and its relevance to the PICO(TT) question.
- Locate search terms in MeSH or CINAHL tree structure and uses database limiters to conduct search. (Restrict to major topic, include terms lower on the hierarchy, subheadings.)

- Find an article on a nursing theory and how it is applied to a specific population.
- Examine the references in an article relevant to the PICO(TT) question and identify additional articles that relate to the research question.
- Use database limiters to locate a variety of material within parameters given in a worksheet (e.g., a systematic review on a topic that is more than 3 years old, a clinical trial on humans).
- Demonstrate using limiters in PubMed/Medline and CINAHL to narrow search (e.g., publication type, publication factors such as language, population factors, such as age groups).
- Establish an account in NCBI and CINAHL to save searches, set up alerts, and save search history.
- Conduct a literature review, systematic review, metaanalysis, or metasynthesis to determine contradictions or unique characteristics of the research to guide nursing practice.
- Demonstrate the difference in results found using the same search terms in different databases (for instance, searching the term "neoplasms" in Medline/PubMed and CINAHL).

REFERENCES

American Association of Colleges of Nursing. (2006a). *The essentials of doctoral educaton for advanced nursing practice*. Retrieved from http://www.aacn.nche.edu/dnp/Essentials.pdf Accessed April 9, 2017.

American Association of Colleges of Nursing. (2006b). *Nursing research*. Retrieved from http://www.aacn.nche.edu/publications/position/NsgResearch.pdf.

American Association of Colleges of Nursing. (2008). *The essentials of baccalaureate education for professional nursing practice*. Retrieved from http://www.aacn.nche.edu/education-resources/BaccEssentials08.pdf.

American Association of Colleges of Nursing. (2010). *The Research-Focused Doctoral Program in Nursing: Pathways to Excellence*. Retrieved from http://www.aacn.nche.edu/education-resources/PhDPosition.pdf.

American Association of Colleges of Nursing. (2011). *The essentials of master's education in nursing*. Retrieved from http://www.aacn.nche.edu/education-resources/MastersEssentials11.pdf.

American Nurses Association. (2015). *Nursing: scope and standards of practice*. Retrieved from https://www.r2library.com/Resource/Title/1558106197.

Association of College & Research Libraries. (2016). *Framework for information literacy for higher education*. Retrieved from http://www.ala.org/acrl/sites/ala.org.acrl/files/content/issues/infolit/Framework_ILHE.pdf.

Association of College & Research Libraries 2013 *The information literacy competency standards for nursing*. Retrieved from <http://www.ala.org/acrl/standards/nursing> Accessed 04.19.17.

Costa, L. & Poe, S. S. 2012 Evidence appraisal: Research In Dearholt, S. L. & Dang, D. (Eds.), *Johns Hopkins Nursing Evidence-Based Practice* (pp. 83–124). Retrieved from http://ntserver1.wsulibs.wsu.edu:2362/lib/wsu/reader.action?docID=3383920# Accessed 05.03.17.

Cronenwett, L., Sherwood, G., Barnsteiner, J., Disch, J., Johnson, J., & Mitchell, P. (2007). Quality and safety education for nurses. *Nursing Outlook, 55*(3), 122–131.

Davies, K. S. 2011. Formulating the evidence based practice question: A review of the frameworks. *Evidence Based Library and Information Practice, 6* 2, 75–80. Retrieved from https://journals.library.ualberta.ca/eblip/index.php/EBLIP/article/viewFile/9741/8144 Accessed 04.22.17.

Dunning, M., Lugon, M. & MacDonald, J. 1998 Is clinical effectiveness a management issue? *British Medical Journal, 316* 7127 243–244. Retrieved from https://www.ncbi.nlm.nih.gov/pmc/articles/PMC2665502/pdf/9472497.pdf Accessed 05.14.17.

Health Sciences Interest Group. (2013). *Teaching tips - Mapping to the ACRL information literacy competency standards for nursing.* Retrieved from https://healthsciencesinterestgroup.wikispaces.com/Teaching+Tips+-+Mapping+to+the+ACRL+Information+Literacy+Competency+Standards+for+Nursing.

International Council of Nurses. (2012). *Closing the gap: From evidence to action.* Geneva, Switzerland. Retrieved from http://www.nursingworld.org/MainMenuCategories/ThePracticeofProfessionalNursing/Improving-Your-Practice/Research-Toolkit/ICN-Evidence-Based-Practice-Resource/Closing-the-Gap-from-Evidence-to-Action.pdf.

Jones, K. R. (2010). Rating the level, quality, and strength of the research evidence. *Journal of Nursing Care Quality, 25*(4), 304–400. https://doi.org/10.1097/NCQ.06013e381db8a44.

Melnyk, B., Gallagher-Ford, L., & Fineout-Overholt, E. (2017). *Implementing the evidence-based practice (EBP) competencies in healthcare: A practical guide for improving quality, safety, and outcomes.* Indianapolis, IN: Sigma Theta Tau International.

Ramer, S. L. (2005). Site-ation pearl growing: Methods and librarianship history and theory. *Journal of the Medical Library Association, 93*(3), 397–400.

Royal College of Nursing. (2011). *RCN competencies: Finding, using and managing information: Nursing, midwifery, health and social care information literacy competencies.* Retrieved from https://www2.rcn.org.uk/__data/assets/pdf_file/0005/276449/003053.pdf.

Stevens, K. R. (2005). *Essential competencies for evidence-based practice in nursing.* San Antonio, TX: Academic Center for Evidence-Based Practice.

CHAPTER 7

Evaluation of Information

Sue F. Phelps
Washington State University, Vancouver, WA, United States

Nowhere is the evaluation of information more important than it is in the practice of health care. Patients have every right to expect that the treatment they receive is based on good scientific evidence and that the practitioner caring for them is using the most current and reliable information possible to make health care decisions. Though it is a common practice in higher education to assess scholarship on the merits of the author of the work and their expertise and experience in addressing a specific topic, this method does not suffice for the evaluation of health sciences literature. There are some instances where looking at authority applies to the health sciences but more often the criterion for assessment of medical information is far more complex. Nurses wanting to improve their practice by seeking the best evidence available are charged with scrutinizing the many factors related to the research methodology beyond that of the authority of the researchers. This chapter discusses a range of evaluation techniques depending on the information need of the nurse and the type of information required.

7.1 FRAMEWORK FOR INFORMATION LITERACY FOR HIGHER EDUCATION

The ACRL Framework, as a guide to higher education in general, addresses the evaluation of information primarily through the lens of authority but allows for flexibility depending on the community of the user and their information need.

> Information resources reflect their creators' expertise and credibility and are evaluated based on the information need and the context in which the information will be used. Authority is constructed in that various communities may recognize different types of authority. It is contextual in that the information need may help to determine the level of authority required.

> *(ACRL, 2016, p. 4).*

Two salient concepts in this description for nursing community in recognizing authority are the context of the information need and how the information is constructed. The context for nursing can range from personal information gathering to practice changing research. The evaluation criteria are commensurate with the information need. If the context of the information need does not involve practice change, the source of the information may be the best evaluation criteria.

For questions that require the best evidence for practice the nurse will most often seek out the most recent research which is found in journal publications. The evaluation of research reports cannot rely solely on the reputation of those conducting the research but must look at how the information was constructed. More advanced nurses will evaluate the research methods used to come to conclusions before implementing changes in patient care or practice procedures.

The Framework acknowledges that "novice learners may need to rely on basic indicators of authority, such as type of publication or author credentials, where experts recognize schools of thought or discipline-specific paradigms" (ACRL, 2016, p. 4). The evaluation of information is developmental in the profession and consistent with the level of education and responsibility.

The knowledge practices of this frame also stress attention to bias, "especially in terms of others' worldviews, gender, sexual orientation, and cultural orientations" (ACRL, 2016, p. 4) stating learners who are developing in this area should strive to keep an open mind, assess content with a skeptical view while keeping their own biases and world view in mind. They further suggest that in order to maintain this attitude that frequent self-evaluation is required. This concept of openness to world views and cultural orientations is a hallmark of evidence-based practice where patient values and preferences are an element of health care decision-making (Melnyk & Fineout-Overholt, 2011). The Royal College of Nursing Competencies admonish the nurse to "judge when and how [a nurse's] own biases and cultural context are influencing how the information is perceived and interpreted" (RCN, 2011, p. 8) as well.

7.2 INFORMATION LITERACY COMPETENCY STANDARDS FOR NURSING

The Information Literacy Competency Standards for Nursing (ILCSN) put into operation the concepts and knowledge practices of the Framework. They delineate elements of the Framework and the standards that can be used for evaluation of information as well as evaluation of how students and practicing nurses understand the concepts of information appraisal. Standard One of the ILCSN focuses on how the information need determines the type of information and the level of authority required for evaluation. Standard Three addresses the construction of information in the research including the matter of bias as it relates to the research methodology.

7.2.1 The Context of the Information Need

The ILCSN Standard One, states "[T]the information literate nurse determines the nature and extent of the information needed." More specifically, they detail "[T]the information literate nurse identifies a variety of types and formats of potential sources for information" (ACRL, 2013).

Questions which do not involve practice change or patient care can often be satisfied with an answer that is less rigorous in content or creation. A simple curiosity or exploration at the beginning of a research project can often be satisfied by an entry in a text book, an encyclopedia, or with a well-informed Internet search. Identifying likely types of publications where appropriate information is published is necessary to fulfilling any information need. Can the question be answered in a popular publication or would the answer more likely be found in a trade journal? Some questions may be historical in nature and require a seminal article or monograph while others call for current data. Regardless of the source, the information literate nurse will ask themselves if the author or source of the information is qualified to speak to a subject. This is when authority, whether by the author's personal qualifications, the organization they represent, or the references that they cite, lend credibility to the information.

If the information need is general in nature and the goal is for the nurse to familiarize themselves with a new health issue or medication a reliable website, such as MedlinePlus.gov, would be an adequate information source drawing its authority from the National Institute of Health. Organizational websites such as the National Cancer Society or the American Lung Association as well as Medline Plus are information resources appropriate for general knowledge or patient education, drawing their reliability from their mission, board of directors, and history of trustworthiness. Publications from, or recommended by, various nursing professional organizations is another rich source of material, as well. For nurses who have access to some medical databases a good source of basic information are the Cumulative Index to Nursing and Allied Health Literature (CINAHL) evidence-based care sheets. These two page summaries with references to research studies and evidence codes for quick information updates are useful for nurses or for patient education. They draw on the authority of the care sheet authors, reviews, and editor of the CINAHL Information Systems.

The ILCSN stress that the nurse be able to distinguish between facts, opinion, and points of view and should be able to recognize "assumptions, prejudice, deception, or manipulation in [the] information" or in how the information is used (ACRL, 2013). Blogs for instance may be a viable way to keep up on the most recent thinking of scientists, practitioners, or librarians but they are also a place where opinions can be published without evidence. Opinion pieces in professional journals are not usually based on research but may be cutting edge thinking. Nurses, as well as all readers, must apply a critical eye to all information. Research reports may contain bias in the text of the report or it may be embedded in the application of the methodology. For instance, studies about medication that are sponsored by pharmaceutical companies or treatments strongly advocated by authors offering skewed evidence are identifiable by nursing students and nurses at every level of practice.

7.2.2 Preappraised Evidence

Most practicing nurses, unless they are attached to a research institution or teaching hospital, do not have access to the same range of medical databases as those who are and therefore do not have access to all of the most recent research reports. It raises the question, then, where do nurses go to look for practice evidence? In the current climate of information overload, how can they be assured that the information they are getting is credible, reliable, valid, accurate, and has a minimum of bias? Cheeseman (2013) describes preappraised evidence sources available to the practicing nurse that "have undergone a filtering process to include only those studies that are of high quality... and are regularly updated so that the evidence accessed through these sources is current" (Cheeseman, 2013, p. 127). These sources can be evaluated following the 6S Model of preappraised evidence which describes a hierarchy to aid in selecting an information source. See Fig. 7.1 for levels of evidence.

Systems is at the peak of the evidence model where characteristics of the individual patient are automatically linked to the current best evidence via a computerized decision support system and the clinician is informed of key aspects of how to manage patient treatment. If systems are not in place the next layer of the 6S model is Summaries. This includes a number of point-of-care proprietary databases that may be provided by a hospital or clinic,

Searching for evidence

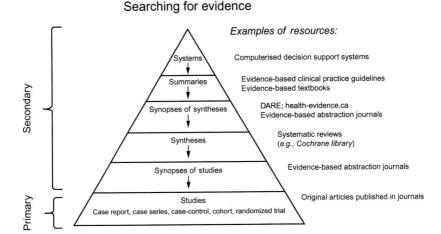

DiCenso A, Bayley L, Haynes RB. Accessing preappraised evidence: fine-tuning the 5S model into a 6S model. ACP Journal Club, 2009

Fig. 7.1 Searching for Evidence. (Reprinted with permission.) DiCenso, Bayley, and Haynes (2009) recommend that the search for information start at the highest level possible, the Systems layer. This is a computerized decision support system (CDSS) that is linked to an electronic health record. It integrates and summarizes all relevant and up to date research about a given clinical problem (Cheeseman, 2013; Ciliska, Jull, & Thompson, 2009) using data from the treating clinicians, laboratory reports, imaging reports, and pharmacy systems. Though this is seen as the highest level of preappraised evidence, Cheeseman (2013) reports that considerable development is needed before the current best evidence is integrated into the electronic health records.

the most well known of which are DynaMed and UpToDate. Each is designed to provide point of care medical information that is easy to use and available on a portable device. Each product has an explicit review process and a high level of currency. A more affordable product for individuals who do not have access to the more expensive summary products is epocrates or epocrates Plus medical reference application (http://www.epocrates.com/). Ciliska et al. (2009) also recommend evidence-based textbooks as a source of reliable medical information in the Summaries category.

The next level on the hierarchy is Synopses of Syntheses. A Synthesis is more commonly known as a systematic review and is an organized method used to gather all related research evidence on a given question based on strict inclusion criteria. The results are described qualitatively in a metaanalysis or qualitatively, and conclusions are made. This saves the clinician vast amounts of time and gives them the assurance that the research has undergone the evaluation of their peers. The synopsis of syntheses summarizes the findings of high-quality systematic reviews and can be found in evidence-based abstraction journals.

If there is no synopsis available then Syntheses are the next level of hierarchy and can be found in the Cochrane Library (http://www.cochranelibrary.com/) or the Joanna Briggs Institute Library of Systematic Reviews (http://journals.lww.com/jbisrir/pages/default.aspx). For nurses who have access to the Medline or CINAHL databases, systematic reviews can be found indexed there using the database limiters.

If syntheses of multiple studies are not available, then Synopses of a Single Study will provide an overview of the study along with a commentary and can be found in evidence-based practice journals. In some cases that can be enough information to inform clinical practice. There is value to a Synopsis of a Single Study over a Single Study because the research had to be considered of clinical relevance for it to be considered for review and the quality of the methodology to merit a synopsis. The commentary also gives it additional value (Cheeseman, 2013). Single research studies should be appraised according to their accuracy, credibility, validity, reliability, level of evidence, and its relevance to the clinical question at hand. Because summaries, syntheses, and synopses take time as does the publication process the information may not be the most recent. Research articles are likely to be the most up to date information available.

7.2.3 Credibility in the Construction of Information

Standard Three of the ILCSN states, "The information literate nurse critically evaluates the procured information and its sources…" and states the nurse "[S]selects information by articulating and applying criteria for evaluating both the information and its sources" (ACRL, 2013). The source, in the case of medical literature, is the research that brought about new information, or an article that confirms the findings of a previous study. It is requisite that the nurse who makes changes in practice be able to decipher the many elements of the research report. As stated earlier, single research studies should be appraised according to their accuracy, credibility, validity, reliability, level of evidence, and its relevance to the clinical question at hand. A quick and simple way of assessing research studies is by use of one of the several models that illustrate the levels of evidence a nurse might find in the literature.

7.2.3.1 Levels of Evidence

The *Evidence Pyramid* is commonly used in medical education to determine the level of evidence. It places opinion and background information at the

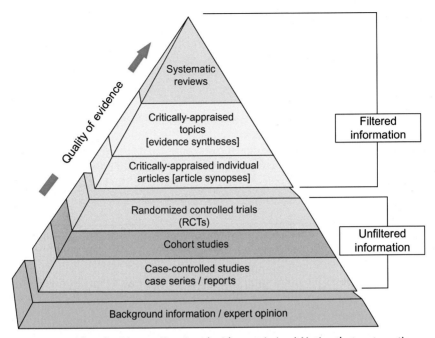

Fig. 7.2 Hierarchy of evidence. (Reprinted with permission.) Notice that systematic reviews, particularly quantitative reviews, are at the top of the evidence pyramid. Ingham-Broomfield (2016) calls them the most reliable of all of the study types and the highest standard in evidence-based care. Just below that on the pyramid are evidence syntheses which offer a summary of related studies. They do not have the rigor of a systematic review and lack standardization of the studies included in the review, but their advantage is in the analysis and interpretation of the selected studies. Also, similar to the pre-appraised study hierarchy, the next level of evidence is an article synopses. It has the benefit of an expert defining the article strengths but is less reliable than the evidence syntheses of more than one article. These first three research methods are considered filtered information according to this pyramid because they have undergone a level of appraisal. The last four are unfiltered. Of those the randomized controlled trial is called the gold standard and is considered very reliable. Next are cohort studies followed by case series and case reports with editorials, opinions, ideas, and anecdotes as the least reliable level of evidence (Ingham-Broomfield, 2016).

bottom of the pyramid, not excluding it from consideration for some information needs, and progresses through the higher qualities of evidence to systematic reviews for the highest level of clinical decision-making. The pyramid in Fig. 7.2 is familiar to nursing students and most frequently used by librarians in teaching evaluation of research evidence. It is easily applied by less advanced nurses.

Melnyk and Fineout-Overholt offer other version in Table 7.1 of the hierarchy with more emphasis placed on specific research methods and dividing

Table 7.1 Rating system for the hierarchy of evidence

Level I: Evidence from a systematic review of all relevant randomized controlled trials (RCT's), or evidence-based clinical practice guidelines based on systematic reviews of RCTs

Level II: Evidence obtained from at least one well-designed Randomized Controlled Trial (RCT)

Level III: Evidence obtained from well-designed controlled trials without randomization, quasiexperimental

Level IV: Evidence from well-designed case-control and cohort studies

Level V: Evidence from systematic reviews of descriptive and qualitative studies

Level VI: Evidence from a single descriptive or qualitative study

Level VII: Evidence from the opinion of authorities and/or reports of expert committees

Melnyk, B. M., & Fineout-Overholt, E. (2005). Evidence-based practice in nursing and healthcare: A guide to best practice. Lippincott Williams & Wilkins, Philadelphia, p. 10, Reprinted with permission.

systematic reviews into two categories, one for reviews of randomized controlled trials and one for reviews of qualitative studies. Melnyk and Fineout-Overholt combine case-controlled studies and cohort studies while the evidence pyramid considers the cohort study to be stronger evidence.

The Johns Hopkins Model describes five levels of evidence adding quality guides for each type of information. The quality guides are specific to each type of evidence in the hierarchy, and though they are brief, they are descriptive enough for a beginning nurse to parse out the strength of the evidence. According to Schaffer, Sandau, and Diedrick (2003) it is the clearest criterion for evaluating the quality of the evidence, and along with the evidence rating scale, it is the most helpful for baccalaureate and master's level students. The Johns Hopkins model is shown in Table 7.2.

Bandolier, an independent journal about evidence-based healthcare, written by Oxford scientists, offers the simplest method of appraisal. They recommend medical practitioners keep the following in mind when evaluating research:

- *Quality*—Trials that are randomized and double blind, to avoid selection and observer bias, and where we know what happened to most of the subjects in the trial.
- *Validity*—Trials that mimic clinical practice, or could be used in clinical practice, and with outcomes that make sense. For instance, in chronic disorders we want long-term, not short-term trials. We are [also] … interested in outcomes that are large, useful, and statistically very significant ($p < 0.01$, a 1 in 100 chance of being wrong).

Table 7.2 Johns Hopkins nursing evidence-based practice, Appendix C: Evidence level and quality guide

Evidence levels	Quality guides
Level I Experimental study, randomized controlled trial (RCT) Systematic review of RCTs, with or without metaanalysis **Level II** Quasiexperimental study Systematic review of a combination of RCTs and quasiexperimental, or quasiexperimental studies only, with or without metaanalysis **Level III** Nonexperimental study Systematic review of a combination of RCTs, quasiexperimental and nonexperimental studies, or nonexperimental studies only, with or without metaanalysis Qualitative study or systematic review with or without a metasynthesis	(A) High quality: Consistent, generalizable results; sufficient sample size for the study design; adequate control; definitive conclusions; consistent recommendations based on comprehensive literature review that includes thorough reference to scientific evidence (B) Good quality: Reasonably consistent results; sufficient sample size for the study design; some control, fairly definitive conclusions; reasonably consistent recommendations based on fairly comprehensive literature review that includes some reference to scientific evidence (C) Low quality or major flaws: Little evidence with inconsistent results; insufficient sample size for the study design; conclusions cannot be drawn

Continued

Table 7.2 Johns Hopkins nursing evidence-based practice, Appendix C: Evidence level and quality guide—cont'd

Evidence levels	Quality guides
Level IV Opinion of respected authorities and/or nationally recognized expert committees/consensus panels based on scientific evidence Includes: • Clinical practice guidelines • Consensus panels	(A) High quality: Material officially sponsored by a professional, public, private organization, or government agency; documentation of a systematic literature search strategy; consistent results with sufficient numbers of well-designed studies; criteria-based evaluation of overall scientific strength and quality of included studies and definitive conclusions; national expertise is clearly evident; developed or revised within the last 5 years (B) Good quality: Material officially sponsored by a professional, public, private organization, or government agency; reasonably thorough and appropriate systematic literature search strategy; reasonably consistent results, sufficient numbers of well-designed studies; evaluation of strengths and limitations of included studies with fairly definitive conclusions; national expertise is clearly evident; developed or revised within the last 5 years (C) Low quality or major flaws: Material not sponsored by an official organization or agency; undefined, poorly defined, or limited literature search strategy; no evaluation of strengths and limitations of included studies, insufficient evidence with inconsistent results, conclusions cannot be drawn; not revised within the last 5 years

Level V

Based on experiential and nonresearch evidence

Includes:

- Literature reviews
- Quality improvement, program, or financial evaluation
- Case reports
- Opinion of nationally recognized experts(s) based on experiential evidence

Organizational Experience:

(A) High quality: Clear aims and objectives; consistent results across multiple settings; formal quality improvement, financial or program evaluation methods used; definitive conclusions; consistent recommendations with thorough reference to scientific evidence

(B) Good quality: Clear aims and objectives; consistent results in a single setting; formal quality improvement or financial or program evaluation methods used; reasonably consistent recommendations with some reference to scientific evidence

(C) Low quality or major flaws: Unclear or missing aims and objectives; inconsistent results; poorly defined quality improvement, financial or program evaluation methods; recommendations cannot be made

Literature Review, Expert Opinion, Case Report, Community Standard, Clinician Experience, Consumer Preference:

(A) High quality: Expertise is clearly evident; draws definitive conclusions; provides scientific rationale; thought leader(s) in the field

(B) Good quality: Expertise appears to be credible; draws fairly definitive conclusions; provides logical argument for opinions

(C) Low quality or major flaws: Expertise is not discernible or is dubious; conclusions cannot be drawn

©The Johns Hopkins Hospital/The Johns Hopkins University, Reprinted with permission.

- *Size*—Trials (or collections of trials) that have large numbers of patients, to avoid being wrong because of the random play of chance.

"These are the criteria on which we should judge evidence. For it to be strong evidence, it has to fulfill the requirements of all three criteria."

(Bandolier)

7.2.3.2 Appraising the Research Report

When more advanced nurses are evaluating research studies they will carry out a more granular assessment of research reports looking at the details of each study's methodology, first asking if the clinical question of the study matches the research design. According to "Supporting Clinical Care: An Institute in Evidence-Based Practice for Medical Librarians (SCC)" the following in Table 7.3 are the best types of studies for the following question types (SCC, 2016).

Notice that the only preferred method for evaluating a medical intervention for therapy is a randomized controlled trial and for a question involving a diagnostic test the best study is independent, blind comparison to a gold standard. However, a prognosis, harm/etiology, or a prevention question have more than one type of study that will address the research question. Not only this is an important ingredient when evaluating research studies, but it can also be very helpful when advanced practice nurses are planning original research projects.

Having determined if the research method matches the research question the nurse can then assess the strength of the evidence, looking for accuracy and credibility; validity; and reliability; as well as whether the research is relevant to the question they wish to address. Credibility is demonstrated by

Table 7.3 In each case, a systematic review of all the available studies is better than an individual study. A systematic review will compare several appropriately designed studies that have looked at the same question and aggregate the results (SCC, 2016)

Question type	Study type: most preferred listed first
Therapy	Randomized Control Trial (RCT)
Diagnostic test	Independent, blind comparison to gold standard
Prognosis	Cohort study > case control > case series
Harm/etiology	RCT > cohort study > case control > case series
Prevention	RCT > cohort study > case control
Cost-effectiveness	Economic analysis
Quality of life	Qualitative study

accuracy and validity recorded in the actions of the research, expression of opinions, and transparency of research biases.

Validity refers to whether the results of a study are obtained through sound scientific methods with bias and confounding variables considered (Melnyk & Fineout-Overholt, 2011). Nurses should look for studies with randomization of the subjects selected so that any differences can be attributed to the effect of the treatment intervention. They will check to see that the baseline characteristics of the subjects are similar and that subjects, health workers, and those involved in the study are blinded to equalize expectations of everyone involved. Advanced nurses will look for indications that the treatment group and the control group are treated equally and that all subjects who entered a research study are accounted for. Dropouts or those who cannot be found for follow-up may disrupt the balance created through randomization and cause differences between groups that affect study outcomes (SCC, 2016).

Reliability refers to whether the interventions described as the results of study will have the same effect when used again. Studies that have been replicated with the same results are an indicator of high reliability as are systematic reviews of the same intervention with consistent results across studies. In conjunction with assessing for bias nurses should look for whether researchers took into consideration the possible confounding variables in their research design, data analysis, and interpretation of the data (Melnyk & Fineout-Overholt, 2011). Finally, the nurse needs to address the simple question, "will the results of the study help me to take care of my patient or improve my practice?" Are these study results going to generalize to my workplace; will they apply to my patient's situation; is the intervention going to be one that will fit the cultural/family/belief system I am trying to effect?

7.2.3.3 Multidisciplinary Research

There are times that questions arise which may be outside of the health care field and cannot be answered by the usual medical resources. ILCSN state that the nurse "Identifies the various disciplines publishing research on the concepts of the question (e.g., health sciences, biology, psychology)" and "Considers resources from a variety of disciplines beyond nursing, including education and teaching, psychology, business, leadership and management, public health, health care administration, demographics, and social sciences" (ACRL, 2013). This skill is particularly important for students or researchers who are seeking to answer questions of interest in multiple disciplines.

Questions regarding treating anorexia would certainly not only require medical intervention but also require information relating to psychology. For a young person there would be questions of learning and education. Knowing how to find information outside of the usual nursing and medical resources is requisite to providing comprehensive treatment. Additionally, the ILCSN suggests that nurses make themselves aware of experts in their area of interest remembering that researchers are usually happy to talk about their work. Experts can be found through their published work or through professional associations and since contact information is included in most research articles there is built in access for anyone who is interested. For nurses with a research focus this is also a way to build a network of colleagues who share the same research interests.

7.3 PROGRESSION OF NURSING EDUCATION AND PRACTICE

7.3.1 The Quality and Safety Education for Nurses Prelicensure

Nurses, from the very beginning of their training, are expected to demonstrate knowledge, skills, and attitudes (KSAs) regarding the authority and credibility of information as they are expressed in the ACRL Framework and ILCSN. In the Quality and Safety Education for Nurses (QSEN) standards (Cronenwett et al., 2007) include the need for nurses to be able to "describe how diverse cultural, ethnic, and social backgrounds function as sources of patient, family, and community values" in order to provide patient centered care. The skill required to gain this information is demonstrated in the clinical interview with the patient and his/her families (Cronenwett et al., 2007). In addition, nurses may increase their understanding of various ethnic and cultural groups by exploring websites, books, and other material remaining aware of the authority of the information regardless of the format. The QSEN knowledge and skills also extend to the research literature under the requirements for evidence-based practice (Cronenwett et al., 2007).

7.3.2 The Essentials of Baccalaureate Education for Professional Nursing Practice

The Essentials of Baccalaureate Education for Professional Nursing Practice addresses authority and credibility under Essential III: Scholarship for Evidence-Based Practice, in saying that "Scholarship for the baccalaureate graduate involves...appraisal and integration of evidence" (AACN, 2008, p. 15) and "provides a basic understanding of how evidence is developed, including the research process…" (p. 16). Additionally, graduates of a baccalaureate program are prepared to evaluate the credibility of sources of information at different levels, for instance, textbooks, case studies, reviews, Internet resources, metaanalysis, or systematic reviews depending on the information need.

7.3.3 The Essentials of Master's Education in Nursing

The Essentials of Master's Level nursing practice retain the skills of the Baccalaureate nurses with the added expectation that they identify problems and gaps in evidence needing answers for clinical practice (AACN, 2011). More specifically, a graduate program should prepare a graduate to "evaluate the credibility of sources of information, including but not limited to databases and Internet resources… [and] to evaluate data from all relevant sources, including technology…" (AACN, 2011, p. 16 and 19). This is expressed as being the responsibility of individuals and members of collaborative treatment teams.

7.3.4 The Essentials of Doctoral Education for Advanced Nursing Practice

The Essentials for Doctors of Nursing Practice state the degree of DNP is built upon the generalist foundation acquired in Baccalaureate and Masters level programs (AACN, 2006). With that foundation in place the DNP graduate program prepares the student to "Use analytic methods to critically appraise existing literature and other evidence to determine and implement the best evidence for practice" (AACN, 2006).

7.4 THE RESEARCH-FOCUSED DOCTORAL PROGRAM IN NURSING: PATHWAYS TO EXCELLENCE

Likewise the Research-Focused Doctoral Program in Nursing is based on the same foundation with the primary expectation of research, scholarship, and dissemination of scholarship. Specific skills and expectations for literature research are not delineated in the report of the AACN task force on the research-focused Doctorate in Nursing.

APPENDIX 7.1. TEACHING TIPS

Nurse educators and nursing librarians can facilitate nursing students learning by using any of the following teaching tips (Health Sciences Interest Group, 2013):

- Analyze patients/persons with conditions first person experiences with our healthcare system. Reflect on how their experience informs your practice.
- Have a panel of "experts" with different personal and professional perspectives (e.g., patient, person with a condition, parent, nurse, advocate, MD, FNP, psychologist, social worker) visit class, and share their knowledge about or experience with the topic. (e.g., children with asthma).
- Evaluate consumer health information sources for accuracy, timeliness, and appropriateness.
- Evaluate a protocol from work and analyze it in class with a worksheet to judge if it is evidence-based or not.
- Provide examples of clinical opinions from research, and evidence summaries. Identify what differentiates them and in what context each would be useful.
- Discuss the possible impact of assumptions, prejudice, deception, and manipulation in the research process. Provide examples of cases studies, such as the historic "Tuskegee Study of Untreated Syphilis in the Negro Male," or research studies funded by pharmaceutical companies. Identify their own biases as researchers and information consumers.
- Identify the context of a current scholarly article and compares it with another source on the same topic from a significantly different historical, social, or cultural context. Discuss the influence of context on the production and interpretation of information in the health professions.
- Identify a popular media article on a health topic and verifies its claims using another source. Describe and critically evaluate the research methods and arguments of both articles.
- Classify evidence-based practice resource on a given topic, using the "Levels of Evidence Pyramid" Report to class the highest-level or most relevant evidence they found, and to explain how it supports a specific practice.
- Validate understanding and interpretation of information through discourse with other BSN students, individuals, subject-area experts, and/or practitioners by:
- Attend or observe ethics rounds, and/or a presentation of an ethics committee member at a hospital.
- Have a fieldwork experience with the goal of partnering with a team in practice, such as a patient safety initiative interdisciplinary team, an interprofessional education team, or a quality improvement team.
- Ask and discuss with multiple professionals about professional roles, knowledge translation, role boundaries, and diverse disciplinary perspectives.

REFERENCES

American Association of Colleges of Nursing. (2006). *The essentials of doctoral education for advanced nursing practice.* Retrieved from http://www.aacn.nche.edu/dnp/Essentials.pdf. Accessed 9 May 2017.

American Association of Colleges of Nursing. (2008). *The essentials of baccalaureate education for professional nursing practice.* Retrieved from http://www.aacn.nche.edu/education-resources/BaccEssentials08.pdf. Accessed April 1, 2017.

American Association of Colleges of Nursing. (2011). *The essentials of master's education in nursing.* Retrieved from http://www.aacn.nche.edu/education-resources/MastersEssentials11.pdf.

Association of College & Research Libraries. (2013). *The information literacy competency standards for nursing.* Retrieved from http://www.ala.org/acrl/standards/nursing.

Association of College & Research Libraries. (2016). *Framework for information literacy for higher education.* Retrieved from http://www.ala.org/acrl/sites/ala.org.acrl/files/content/issues/infolit/Framework_ILHE.pdf.

Cheeseman, S. E. (2013). Information literacy: Foundation for evidence-based practice. *Neonatal Network, 32*(2), 127–131. https://doi.org/10.1891/0730-0832.32.2.127.

Ciliska, D., Jull, A., & Thompson, C. (2009). Assessing pre-appraised evidence: Fine-tuning the 5S model into a 6S model. *Evidence based Nursing, 12*(4), 99–101.

Cronenwett, L., Sherwood, G., Barnsteiner, J., Disch, J., Johnson, J., & Mitchell, P. (2007). Quality and safety education for nurses. *Nursing Outlook, 55*(3), 122–131.

DiCenso, A., Bayley, L., & Haynes, R. B. (2009). Accessing pre-appraised evidence: fine-tuning the 5S model into a 6S model. *Evidence-Based Nursing, 12,* 99–101.

Health Sciences Interest Group. (2013). *Teaching tips—Mapping to the ACRL information literacy competency standards for nursing.* Retrieved from https://healthsciencesinterestgroup.wikispaces.com/Teaching+Tips+-+Mapping+to+the+ACRL+Information+Literacy+Competency+Standards+for+Nursing.

Ingham-Broomfield, R. (2016). A nurses' guide to the hierarchy of research designs and evidence. *Australian Journal of Advanced Nursing, 33*(3), 38–43.

Melnyk, B. M., & Fineout-Overholt, E. (2011). *Evidence-based practice in nursing & healthcare: A guide to best practice* (2nd ed.). Philadelphia, PA: Lippincott, Williams & Wilkins.

Royal College of Nursing. (2011). *RCN competencies: Finding, using and managing information: Nursing, midwifery, health and social care information literacy competencies.* Retrieved from https://www2.rcn.org.uk/__data/assets/pdf_file/0005/276449/003053.pdf.

Schaffer, M. A., Sandau, K. E., & Diedrick, L. (2003). Evidence-based practice models for organizational change: Overview and practical applications. *Journal of Advanced Nursing, 69*(5), 1197–1209. https://doi.org/10.1111/j.1365-2648.2012.06122.x.

Supporting Clinical Care. (2016). *An institute in evidence-based practice for medical librarians.* Aurora, Colorado: Health Sciences Library, University of Colorado, Anschutz Medical Campus. July 14–17, 2016.

FURTHER READING

American Association of Colleges of Nursing. (2006). *The essentials of doctoral education for advanced nursing practice.* Retrieved from http://www.aacn.nche.edu/dnp/Essentials.pdf.

American Association of Colleges of Nursing. (2010). *The research-focused doctoral program in nursing: Pathways to excellence.* Retrieved from http://www.aacn.nche.edu/education-resources/PhDPosition.pdf.

Bandolier: Evidence based thinking about health care. (2007). *Critical appraisal.* Retrieved from http://www.bandolier.org.uk/booth/glossary/Critapp.html.

Ebsco Health. (2017). *The cumulative index to nursing and allied health literature.* Retrieved from https://health.ebsco.com/products/the-cinahl-database.

Johns Hopkins Medicine, Center for Evidence-based Practice. (2017). *Johns Hopkins nursing evidence-based practice Evidence Level and Quality Guide*. Retrieved from http://www.hopkinsmedicine.org/evidence-based-practice/jhn_ebp.html.

Melnyk, B. M., & Fineout-Overholt, E. (2005). *Evidence-based practice in nursing & healthcare: A guide to best practice*. Philadelphia: Lippincott Williams & Wilkins.

University of Colorado Anschutz Medical Campus Health Sciences Library. (2016). *Supporting clinical care: An institute in evidence-based practice for medical librarians*. Retrieved from http://hslibraryguides.ucdenver.edu/ebpml.

US National Library of Medicine. (2017). *Medline plus*. Retrieved from https://medlineplus.gov/.

CHAPTER 8

Integrating Information Literacy into the Academic Curriculum and Nursing Practice

Sue F. Phelps*, Loree Hyde[†]
*Washington State University, Vancouver, WA, United States
[†]Kaiser Permanente, Clackamas, OP, United States

Nursing students are sanctioned by the goals of higher education and professional standards to provide nursing care using the most recent research to inform their practice. Evidence-based practice (EBP) has emerged as an important initiative in healthcare worldwide (Farokhzadian, Khajouei, & Ahmadian, 2015) including nursing. It is incumbent on the institutions that educate nurses at every level to see that they not only learn the tenets of nursing but also learn how to retrieve the best information from available resources and analyze them for application.

Melnyk, FineHolt-Overholt, Stillwell, and Williamson (2010) list seven steps of Evidence-Based Practice (EBP):
- Step Zero—Cultivate a spirit of inquiry
- Step One–Ask the burning question in PICOT format
- Step Two—Search and collect the most relevant and best evidence
- Step Three—Critically appraise the evidence
- Step Four—Integrate all evidence with one's clinical expertise, patient preferences, and values in making a practice decision or change
- Step Five—Evaluate the outcome of the practice decisions or changes based on evidence
- Step Six—Disseminate EBP results
(Melnyk et al., 2010)

Steps one through three of EBP are in alignment with information literacy (IL), defined by the Association of College and Research Libraries (ACRL) as the ability to formulate a question, search for, find, and acquire information and then to use the information responsibly (ACRL, 2000). Because nurse educators must incorporate EBP into the nursing curriculum at all levels of education, it only makes sense that information literacy be included in curriculum at all levels, too. As students obtain advanced degrees and professionals advance in their careers the sophistication and skill level of information access and use also advance requiring ongoing professional development.

8.1 STUDENT INFORMATION LITERACY ATTITUDES AND SKILLS

Lack of confidence and lack of the most basic skills of information seeking (identifying keywords, finding scholarly literature, and accessing the full text of articles) is a common problem that stands in the way of nurses engaging in collecting the best evidence possible (McCulley & Jones, 2013; Molteni & Chan, 2015). It may also explain some of the tendency for nurses to seek help from colleagues or to search the Internet when they have a practice question (McCulley & Jones, 2013).

An integrative literature review to identify the attitudes regarding the use of research and evidence-based practice in undergraduate nursing students found that overall there was a positive attitude regarding the intended use of evidence in their nursing practice (Ryan, 2016). And students with a particular area of interest, greater experience and greater knowledge tended to have a more positive attitude toward the future use of evidence. However a repeated factor in the review was a lack of confidence in their ability to engage with research, even though they believed it would be useful in their practice (Ryan, 2016). This lack of confidence certainly affects their future application of EBP when they are working in the field and acclimating to the workplace environment.

When students first arrive at institutions of higher education in every field it is assumed that they are able, with a brief orientation to the library, to find scholarly material without further instruction. This assumption may inadvertently contribute to the over inflated self-rated ability of many nursing students to conduct scholarly research (Waters, Crisp, Rychetmik, & Barratt, 2009; Ivanitskaya, O'Boyle, & Casey, 2006; Molteni & Chan, 2015). Stombaugh et al. (2013) found that beginning students were not able to search for and retrieve information related to patient care issues and mid-level students were unable to choose appropriate sources to make care decisions. Additionally, they found that senior-level students did not have the skills to evaluate the evidence they retrieved (Stombaugh et al., 2013). It is also worth mentioning that most of the nurse educators in higher education at this time completed their academic work prior to the time when resources were available electronically. They often think of the younger nurses as much more technically savvy than they really are when it comes to academic resources. In many cases these educators would benefit from instruction on how to search the library databases along with their students.

In a study of student reflections, using the 1-min paper following an information literacy workshop, two primary themes emerged. When asked "What did you learn today that you think will be useful in your course work" a search strategy was the most frequently reported theme. Many students indicated they encountered information literacy and EBP for the first time during this workshop. Coming in they were not familiar with search strategies, truncation, PICO questions, medical databases such as PubMed and CINAHL and how to access information through their school's interlibrary loan program (Cobus-Kuo & Waller, 2016).

8.2 TEACHING METHODS FOR EVIDENCE-BASED PRACTICE

In a systematic review of international articles aimed at identifying pedagogical strategies to teach evidence-based practice to bachelor's level nursing students, the researcher found two forms of intervention to facilitate learning. First, interventions to learn information literacy and, second, interventions to learn the research process were considered most important for EBP with information literacy at the core (Aglen, 2016). Even with efforts to teach IL, nurses often do not see the relevance for their practice without prior instruction in how to use evidence. Aglen (2016) states that bachelor level of nursing education should be focused on knowledge related to clinical problems guiding the nurse toward knowledge creation using evidence from many relevant sources, not just research. This underscores the importance of the timing for IL instruction and that it be integrated into clinical coursework. As students identify clinical needs they are motivated toward information seeking, accessing, and evaluating.

Librarians from the United States and Canada conducted a systematic review to seek out the instructional methods used to teach EBP and to identify what methods were most effective toward student learning (Swanberg et al., 2016). A total of 27 studies were selected for inclusion which represented upper-year medical students. The studies addressed one or more steps in the EBP process with the most common being acquiring the best evidence followed by asking an answerable question and PICO question development (Swanberg et al., 2016). Most of the studies used more than one instruction method which included lectures, small group discussions, one-to-one instruction, hands on practice searching in databases in a computer lab, with a few studies about instruction done online. Assessment methods ranged from pre- and posttests to standardized tests or tests designed by individual researchers. No single teaching method stood out as being the most effective in this study (Swanberg et al., 2016). The most important factor is that EBP and IL instruction is present; however the nursing faculty and/or librarian choose to present it.

8.3 EXAMPLES OF INFORMATION LITERACY INTEGRATION

There are many ways that the literature illustrates how educators have integrated information literacy into nursing or other medical programs. Current practice in most colleges and universities is for a librarian to visit classes, at the invitation of the instructor, to talk to the class about library research. This usually occurs sometime during the semester when the class is assigned a research project. Librarians call this a one-shot. In some cases it is a shot in the dark for the librarian who has, at most, one class period to cover skills more suited to multiple episodes of instruction. Close collaboration with the instructor may help to focus the 50-min class visit and good pedagogy will dictate how the time is used. Though students do increase their understanding of library research during a one-shot class there are still many concepts and skills that are not addressed.

A first step on expanding the one-shot librarian visit is described by Boruff and Thomas (2011) in which a librarian led hands on workshop was followed with a graded searching assignment. They report the lecture portion of the workshop covered basic library resources and a demonstration of basic searching skills without adequate time for covering controlled vocabulary or the use of limiters in the Medline database. Even so, scores indicated that this short intervention resulted in 101 of 104 students receiving at least 8 of 10 points on the assignment (Boruff & Thomas, 2011).

Ithica College in New York (Cobus-Kuo & Waller, 2016) implemented a hands-on workshop that is offered once per semester. The 75-min workshop is tailored to a course assignment and focuses on building a good PICO question and finding the best and most current information using basic subject searching, search limiters, publication type, and clinically relevant limiters. Librarians also created a web-based course guide to assist with the assignment (Cobus-Kuo & Waller, 2016). The addition of the website is an excellent supplement to the one-shot workshop allowing students to review concepts as needed to aid learning. Many of the students in the Cobus-Kuo and Waller workshops said that they encountered information literacy and EBP for the first time and reported learning new or improved information literacy skills at this level of intervention (Cobus-Kuo & Waller, 2016).

Demczuk, Gottschalk, and Littleford (2009), two librarians and a doctor, worked together using the Information Literacy Competency Standards for Higher Education (ACRL, 2000) to create nine modules to work into the first 9 months of the anesthesia curriculum, as illustrated in Table 8.1. Each module is a 2-hour hands-on training in small interactive groups. The instructor demonstrates the topic skill and students engage in learning activities to practice that skill which is also based on current learning activities in their clinical work (Demczuk et al., 2009). Because the librarians were working closely with the teaching faculty they were able to make these modules a meaningful learning experience. Students leave the training modules with an assignment and librarians are available for additional consultation.

Nurse educators at Northern Michigan University (NMU) (Flood, Gasiewicz, & Delpier, 2010) who wanted to integrate information literacy into their curriculum found that in 2010 examples in the literature were rare. In response they developed a series of assignments to increase student awareness of the need for information and promote skill development in finding, evaluating, and using information for practice. The assignments were graduated in complexity for novice, intermediate, and advanced students with the goal of preparing BSN graduates for a beginning level of informatics practice and included additional instruction on informatics competencies (Flood et al., 2010).

Table 8.1 Anesthesia clinical assistant program information literacy modules (Demczuk et al., 2009)

Module 1	Orientation to research services and support
Module 2	Formulating a clinical question, Pubmed Searching
Module 3	Introduction to Information Management (Refworks)
Module 4	Advanced Pubmed and Scopus searching
Module 5	Drug information, anesthesiology E-books
Module 6	Web research & evaluation
Module 7	Keeping current, RSS feeds, my NCBI
Module 8	Investigating anesthesia materials and devices
Module 9	Evaluating evidence, summative assessment

The novice student is introduced to the physical and electronic resources of the library and instructed in accessing and evaluating information. Students are then assigned to work in pairs to find a scholarly article and evaluate it using criteria that include authority, credibility, accuracy, objectivity, currency, and applicability to a clinical question. They submit a written review of their article for grading (Flood et al., 2010).

Intermediate students are given an assignment to create a teaching brochure with the information gathered from a graded literature review and present the brochure to the class in order to practice finding, synthesizing, creating, and disseminating information. Next students identify a policy or procedure related to the care of a patient and conduct a literature review to compare current practice to evidence-based practice. The written assignment requires the students to make recommendations for change (Flood et al., 2010). Though the article does not describe the instruction to support this assignment, there is a strong need for nursing students to receive guidance through the process of conducting a literature review. Often instructor provided guidelines are restricted to "scholarly peer-reviewed articles published within the last five years." Nursing students need additional instruction on opposing viewpoints, organization of articles found, synthesis of information, and how to write a summary of the evidence.

The first two levels of assignments at NMU focus on the clinical aspects of information gathering while nurses are focusing on clinic courses. The advanced students focus on their role development as a nurse, so their assignments shift to looking for care information related to the perspective of patients, their families, and health care providers in the community. An assignment for advanced nursing students is designed for nurses completing an externship wherein they identify examples of how health care information is used in a real world setting (Flood et al., 2010). The progression of these assignments supports the increasing sophistication of information literacy required overtime and assures that graduates are prepared to practice with a foundation of evidence in the many aspects of their profession.

Jacobs, Rosenfeld, and Haber (2003) designed a similar program for Master's level nurses. Though the assignments are very similar to those in the BSN program at NMU the IL class content is more advanced. Students are introduced to searching with a controlled vocabulary, looking at method-based strategies for evaluation, exploring statistical resources, searching the Invisible Web, and critical use of website evaluation, as illustrated in Table 8.2. The NMU program and the Jacobs et al. (2003) program together offer a progression of skills within the curriculum in BSN and Masters level

Table 8.2 Model for integrating information literacy into Master's programs core courses (Jacobs et al., 2003)

Course	Class content	Assignment
Leadership for Advanced Professional Practice Leadership, group processes and dynamics, professional communication strategies, and telecommunications in health care setting are addressed	Database search principles • Database coverage, scope, and selection • CINAHL and Medline; interdisciplinary databases (e.g., PsycINFO, SSCI) • Constructing a research question • Selection of search terms; controlled vocabularies (MESH/ subject headings); expanding a search with synonyms, truncation, keywords • Narrowing a search with Boolean logic; categoric limits • Expanding a search with synonyms	Conduct a literature review to retrieve data-based articles to a support a change project that addresses a leadership problem, challenge, or opportunity as it relates to advanced practice nursing
Research in Nursing Exploration of research problems in nursing, appropriate methodologies and designs, and ethical implications	Evidence-based searching • Methodology-based search strategies • Preevaluated literature • Cochrane Database of Systematic Reviews • Clinical guidelines • Evidence-based journals	Identify, critique, and synthesize information considering design methodology, variables, instrumentation, statistical findings, and so forth
Population-Focused Care Critique of research and other evidence is applied to the analysis of population care strategies	Strategies for finding statistical information • Government databases • Statistical Universe • The invisible Web	Conduct literature reviews related to policy analysis and a population health concern

Continued

Table 8.2 Model for integrating information literacy into Master's programs core courses (Jacobs et al., 2003)—cont'd

Course	Class content	Assignment
Science of Unitary Human Beings The philosophic bases of nursing science and its assumptions are examined in the context of contemporary views of science	Interdisciplinary databases; coverage, scope, and selection • PsycINFO; Social Sciences Citation Index • Allied and Alternative Medicine • The invisible Web	Conduct a literature review relevant to a unitary therapeutic intervention
Nursing Issues and Trends Within the Health Care System Analysis of health care system issues and trends, such as capitation, managed care, and health care reimbursement, from historic, political, and development perspectives	Using Web search engines, directories, metasites, metasearch engines • Library resource Web page: http://library.nyu.edu/research/health/issues.html • Evaluating and citing information from the Web	Critical evaluation of a Web site relevant to course content

courses that are relevant to current coursework, build on previous learning, and prepare the student for a practice based on the best evidence.

Since their implementation in 2000 the Information Literacy Competency Standards for Higher Education (*Standards*) from the Association for Research and College Libraries (ACRL) has become widely accepted in the academy as a guide for information literacy (ACRL, 2000). They have been the footing for campus and library learning goals and have provided a structure from which to teach information literacy for academic librarians since their inception. Health sciences librarians that are not connected to a library that also serves a general education population are ordinarily not involved with ACRL and have not been exposed to or officially adopted the *Standards*. However, there is a considerable amount of nursing literature that concerns information literacy which is in alignment with the *Standards*. In 2013 ACRL adopted the Information Literacy Competency Standards for Nursing (ACRL, 2013) contributing groundwork for medical librarians who provide instruction in nursing education and who supervise nurses in an evidence-based practice environment.

The inception of the Framework for Information Literacy in Higher Education (*Framework*) in 2016 (ACRL, 2016) has given librarians a broader and more conceptual view of information literacy. There has been much discussion in the academic library community about the decision of the ACRL board to replace the *Standards* with the *Framework* and how that would translate into the classroom. Franzen and Bannon (2016) have developed a curriculum map that aligns the steps of evidence-based practice with and the *Standards* and the *Framework*. The EBP steps and the *Standards* focus on specific skill development while the *Framework* gives students something broader to consider. This is in concert with the threshold concepts "which are those ideas in any discipline that are passageways or portals to enlarged understanding or ways of thinking and practicing within that discipline" (ACRL, 2016, p. 2) on which the *Framework* was designed.

8.4 THE ROLE OF THE LIBRARIAN

While Swanberg et al. (2016) looked to the literature for instructional methods used to teach EBP they also found four ways in which librarians are involved in evidence-based practice: planning curricula, delivering instruction, assessing student performance, and authoring journal articles on their EBP training experience (Swanberg et al., 2016). Librarians do not engage in these activities without collaboration with the nursing faculty. In most cases libraries have taken the lead in initiating collaboration with nursing faculty as they have with faculty in other disciplines. Nurse educators are often not aware of the many ways the librarians in their institutions are available and able to assist them with instruction. Promotion from the library is imperative.

8.5 PROFESSIONAL PRACTICE, LOREE HYDE

Just as evidence-based practice and its information literacy components have become consistent fundamentals of nursing education, credentialing and nursing professional practice organizations now specify that evidence-based practice in nursing is an expectation of a professional nursing practice environment (Duphily, 2016; Hain & Kear, 2015). It is well established that EBP is required to provide quality nursing care, making it essential that "all nurses receive the appropriate training and are confident in their abilities to evaluate research and implement evidence-based change" (Mallion & Brooke, 2016, p. 153). Evaluating literature is just one piece of the Information

Literacy process that supports EBP. It is similarly understood that without applying the information literacy-based methods of inquiry, location, critical appraisal, synthesis, and utilization, it would be difficult to realize evidence-based practice (Forster, 2013; Tanner, Pierce, & Pravikoff, 2004). With EBP and IL being integrated into nursing education, it would seem safe to assume that new nurses, being given the opportunity to develop information literacy skills in the curriculum, should be prepared for professional practice from an evidence-based perspective. On the contrary, studies have shown that the use of research to support practice is not necessarily the norm, and that having had course content related to information literacy does not mean that the nurse will have, or take the opportunity to employ IL skills. A 2016 metaethnography of new graduate nurses use of knowledge sources determined that of the sample included (analysis of 17 studies and approximately 150 nurses in a variety of settings), new graduate nurses "draw uncritically on the experienced co-worker as primary knowledge source" (Voldbjerg et al., 2017, p. 1762). In the *Journal of Advanced Nursing*, Forsman et al. reported that for over 2600 nurses transitioning into practice in Sweden, their use of research was "relatively low during the first two years after graduation" and that lack of research utilization continued as a trend past the two-year mark (Forsman, Rudman, Gustavsson, Ehrenberg, & Wallin, 2010, p. 887). In a commentary on the same study, Stilwell credits the research with illustrating the "disconnect between nursing education and clinical practice" and epitomizing the gap between research and practice (Stillwell, 2010, p. 104). The International Council of Nurses have recognized evidence-based practice as an avenue to diminish the theory to practice gap, and cite benefits beyond the support of clinical decision making as improved patient safety and cost reduction (International Council of Nurses, 2012). To address this gap and understand IL in professional practice, we must first examine the barriers to EBP.

8.6 BARRIERS TO EVIDENCE-BASED PRACTICE

In recent years, nurses have moved toward EBP and IL in professional practice to improve outcomes by using evidence to change practice (Hain & Kear, 2015). While nurses' knowledge of EBP and utilization of information literacy skills are increasing, the barriers to implementation are still often documented in the EBP literature (Mallion & Brooke, 2016; Gardner et al., 2016). Mallion and Brooke identified that "the main barriers reported by nurses to implement EBP remain unchanged and include lack of time, knowledge, and skills. Other barriers reported by nurses included a lack of resources, organization support, and the authority to change clinical practice" (p. 152). In another study in consideration of implementing and sustaining EBP, Gardner adds that nurses may not understand the utility EBP or its immediate application to their work (Gardner et al., 2016).

It is of no surprise that lack of time is the most commonly cited barrier to implementing EBP (Duphily, 2016; Forsman et al., 2010; Hosking et al., 2016; Middlebrooks, Carter-Templeton, & Mund, 2016; Shaffer et al., 2013). With increases in high patient acuity and complex patient needs, it is difficult for nurses to prioritize, and EBP may not rank highly when they are able to set priorities (Hosking et al., 2016). Typical nursing workloads and workflows do not build in time to consider practice changes through an EBP lens and work through the process of finding and considering how to best utilize relevant research in practice (Mallion & Brooke, 2016; Middlebrooks et al., 2016; Thomas, 2017).

Access and technology challenges can also prevent nurses from applying information literacy skills in pursuit of EBP. In their review of the literature, Mallion and Brooke found that access to networked, internet-enabled computers, as well as access to libraries, facilitated EBP. If computers that are configured for online research or organizing and storing relevant evidence are not available, even when a nurse does find the time to seek evidence to fulfill an information need, they may not be able to. While the development of clinical medical applications for mobile phones and tablets has grown, lack of mobile technology and wireless connectivity have been shown to prevent the utilization of these evidence-based practice resources by nurses, especially at the point of care, where it could be easier to undertake if the infrastructure was in place (Mackey & Bassendowski, 2017).

Other barriers to accessing online information to inform practice land firmly in the realm of information literacy proficiency and skill. Critical appraisal and synthesis appear to be a point of deficit when it comes to utilizing research in pursuit of EBP (Mallion & Brooke, 2016). Renolen and Hjalmhult uncovered the main concern to the nurses they studied as determining what "knowledge" could be considered evidence and how to incorporate examples from the three commonly identified EBP domains, "knowledge from experience, from science, and from the patient in the situation" (Renolen & Hjälmhult, 2015, p. 636). They found that the nurses relied on experience rather than research literature because they lacked training in information literacy skills and found the use of resources such as bibliographic databases too challenging. While this could again indicate technology issues, it also points to the fact that information literacy skills are not ubiquitous, and that the need to continue IL training and education in the clinical setting should be a priority.

Nurses who are able to overcome the barriers of time and technology, and have gained IL skills, may still continue to deem turning to the literature unnecessary (Middlebrooks et al., 2016). This attitude toward scientific evidence, along with resistance to change, are also common barriers. In a study by Thompson, Aitken, Doran, and Dowding (2013) it was again observed that nurses use experience and advice from their colleagues to guide their practice which may not be rooted in evidence. Many nurses continue to rely on observation or a culture of "we've always done it this way" instead of EBP (Hain & Kear, 2015).

8.7 ORGANIZATIONAL APPROACHES TO EVIDENCE-BASED PRACTICE

A lack of organizational focus on EBP is the barrier that has been most proactively addressed in nursing practice. The expectation of evidence-based practice for any nurse is only realistic if they are working in a setting that promotes and fosters EBP. In an environment that values EBP, nursing leaders will have worked to "build an organizational infrastructure that supports innovation, dissemination of information, care transformation, value- and evidence-based decision making, and long-term sustainability" (Meredith, Cohen, & Raia, 2010, p. 55). A proactive EBP culture promotes critical thinking and the use of evidence in a variety of forms (Voldbjerg, 2016). Other facilitators of success in implementing an ethos of evidence-based practice are also well documented in the literature and include:
- Cultivating an organizational spirit of inquiry
- Securing a commitment from nurse leaders to EBP
- Fostering acceptance and support of EBP from colleagues
- Establishing EBP champions to help develop and sustain staff interest
- Collaborating with library staff to provide EBP and IL education
- Providing financial support for EBP projects
- Empowering the authority to change practice
  (Garland Baird & Miller, 2015; Gerrish & Cooke, 2013; Melnyk, 2016; Solomons & Spross, 2011; Yoder et al., 2014)

With the understanding and identification of these facilitators, healthcare organizations have adopted a variety of programs and practices to bring evidence-based practice to the forefront of patient care. The development of new roles and means of supporting clinical nurses is an acknowledgement that merely addressing the lack of time as a barrier to EBP is "overtly simplistic and logistically unlikely" and that more robust methods are required (Mallion & Brooke, 2016, p. 153). These methods are more systematic and include providing educational courses and programs geared toward EBP, and the development of organizational structure and roles to promote organizational objectives around EBP.

New graduate or new nurse residency programs have been put into place in some healthcare settings with the object of promoting EBP early in a nurse's career. In her article on nursing residency programs, Hosking notes that "new graduates bring fresh knowledge, ideas, and energy to the practice environment and need to be embraced in a culture of EBP" (Hosking et al., 2016, p. 260). Established nurses can harness the momentum of new nurses and will likewise benefit from an atmosphere of critical thinking and questioning practice (Voldbjerg, 2016). These programs also provide the opportunity for librarian led instruction and training, a key component in empowering a spirit of inquiry and building "EBP literacy" skills (Jackson, 2016, p. 278).

The implementation of nursing councils designed to engage, empower, and support participation in EBP is another organizational approach to culture change (McKeever et al., 2016). These councils vary by name, including "Evidence-based Practice," "Research," "Clinical Inquiry," "Clinical Effectiveness," etc. Their exact missions may vary some as well, but typically they share in the goal of promoting evidence-based practice and information literacy, and often include a medical librarian.

Adopting an EBP model is often one of the first activities an EBP council will undertake, as it is extremely useful in providing organizational structure and guidance. A multitude of EBP models exist. In 2013, Stevens identified 47 EBP models, and new models continue to be developed (Goode, Fink, Krugman, Oman, & Traditi, 2011). An EBP Council typically goes through an evaluation process, perhaps using clinical scenarios, to determine which model will best meet their needs. They then introduce it to their organization through educational programs and conferences (Gawlinski & Rutledge, 2008). Their activities can include: identifying opportunities for research as related to institutional priorities; reviewing proposals for research; completing Quality Improvement or EBP projects; and developing educational courses and programs such as EBP and Research fellowships and boot camps, journal clubs, and poster and abstract writing workshops. These councils also contribute to the fulfillment and documentation of the requirements for attaining Magnet designation, should that be a goal of the organization.

Magnet status is a respected distinction a healthcare organization can receive for nursing excellence and quality patient outcomes and is an indicator of an evidence-based practice environment. The American Nurses Credentialing Center's Magnet Recognition Program® takes its name from the inference that the practice environment it requires attracts and retains professional nurses. As Shaffer as wrote in 2013 in her exploration of improving patient care with EBP projects, "the hallmark characteristics of Magnet designation include empowering nurses for autonomous practice and emphasizing critical inquiry, development of new knowledge to improve quality care, and the need to examine and improve outcomes" (Shaffer et al., 2013, p. 354). The American Nursing Credential Center of the American Nurses Association describes Magnet as

> "the highest and most prestigious credential a healthcare organization can achieve fornursing excellence and quality patient care. This performance-driven credential brings   both external prestige and wide-ranging internal benefits, including improved safety, nurse satisfaction and retention, reduced costs, and superior patient outcomes."

(ANCC, 2017, p. 1).

The Magnet Model Component IV, *New Knowledge, Innovations, & Improvements,* as illustrated in Fig. 8.1, is based in research and evidence-based practice and requires that the organization demonstrate their associated

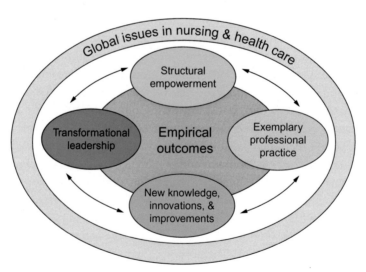

Fig. 8.1 Magnet recognition program: the five model components. *(American Nurses Credentialing Center, 2008, Reprinted with permission.)*

activities (American Nurses Credentialing Center, 2011). The focus within Magnet status on EBP can be generalized to include Information Literacy skills, which are required to acquire, evaluate, and integrate new knowledge into practice.

It is also worth noting that Magnet designated organizations specifically seek out BSN prepared nurses, whom, per a study by Wilson et al. (2015) describing nurses' perceptions of evidence-based practice, report fewer barriers to EBP and possess greater "ability, desire and frequency of behaviors" related to evidence-based practice (Wilson et al., 2015, p. 12). It does appear that BSN-prepared nurses are entering practice better prepared from an evidence-based point of view. Garland et al. found results directly related to BSN prepared nurses as having developed the skills necessary to find research evidence to support their practice (Gardner et al., 2016). Linton et al. discovered similar findings in their 2013 study, revealing that nurses with higher levels of education had greater knowledge of EBP, as well as an attitude toward its implementation (Linton & Prasun, 2013).

Educational programs that promote and provide instruction in information literacy are a large part of EBP council activities. For example, evidence-based practice fellowships that include IL instruction are often a major initiative. In these programs, nurses apply to participate with a proposed EBP or Quality Improvement (QI) project. The EBP model the organization has adopted is used to guide their progress and learning as they develop a PICO question, complete a literature search, appraise and synthesize their evidence, and move forward with a proposal for a practice change. In their study of the effects of educational interventions such as fellowship programs in reducing barriers to EBP, Middlebrooks et al. illustrate the value of Information Literacy in EBP education repeatedly and conclude that "it is clear that approaches such as didactic instruction from an expert in EBP, computer-based instruction especially from a librarian, and EBP projects that allow the nurses to practice the skills they learned have resulted in positive outcomes for participants" (Middlebrooks et al., 2016, p. 404). Overall, fellowships have been shown to be effective in increasing knowledge, skill, and abilities and reducing barriers to EPB (Kim et al., 2017).

It is clear that the relationship between EBP and IL is complex and experienced by nurses in a multitude of ways. Our work on this project recognizes that the role and value of information literacy is central to evidence-based practice, and as Forster states in his phenomenographic exploration of Information Literacy in nursing, both are integral elements of many, if not most, aspects of nursing practice, at any level (Forster, 2013).

REFERENCES

Aglen, B. (2016). Pedagogical strategies to teach bachelor students evidence-based practice: A systematic review. *Nurse Education Today, 36,* 255–263. https://doi.org/10.1016/j.nedt.2015.08.025.

American Nurses Credentialing Center. (2008). *A new model for ANCC's magnet recognition program® [brochure].* Retrieved from http://www.nursecredentialing.org/documents/magnet/newmodelbrochure.aspxAccessed May 3, 2017.

American Nurses Credentialing Center. (2011). *Magnet resource toolkit: Recognizing nursing excellence.* Silver Spring, MD: American Nurses Credentialing Center.

American Nurses Credentialing Center. (2017). *Magnet Recognition Program® Overview.* Retrieved from http://www.nursecredentialing.org/Magnet/ProgramOverview.

Association of College and Research Libraries. (2000). *Information literacy competency standards for higher education.* Retrieved from http://www.ala.org/acrl/standards/informationliteracycompetency.

Association of College & Research Libraries. (2013). *The information literacy competency standards for nursing.* Retrieved from http://www.ala.org/acrl/standards/nursing.

Association of College & Research Libraries. (2016). *Framework for information literacy for higher education.* Retrieved from http://www.ala.org/acrl/sites/ala.org.acrl/files/content/issues/infolit/Framework_ILHE.pdf.

Boruff, J. T., & Thomas, A. (2011). Integrating evidence-based practice and information literacy skills in teaching physical and occupational therapy students. *Health Information and Libraries Journal, 28,* 264–272.

International Council of Nurses 2012 *Closing The Gap: From Evidence to Action* Geneva: International Council of Nurses Retrieved from http://www.nursingworld.org/MainMenuCategories/ThePracticeofProfessionalNursing/Improving-Your-Practice/Research-Toolkit/ICN-Evidence-Based-Practice-Resource/Closing-the-Gap-from-Evidence-to-Action.pdf Accessed 5.1.17.

Cobus-Kuo, L., & Waller, J. (2016). Teaching information literacy and evidence-based practice in an undergraduate speech-language pathology program: A student reflection. *Contemporary Issues in Communication Science and Disorders, 43,* 35–49.

Demczuk, L., Gottschalk, T., & Littleford, J. (2009). Introducing information literacy into anesthesia curricula. *Canadian Journal of Anesthesia/Journal canadien d'anesthésie, 56*(4), 327–335.

Duphily, N. (2016). Linking evidence to practice: A clinical practice guideline project. *NursingPlus Open, 2,* 26–34. https://doi.org/10.1016/j.npls.2016.09.002.

Farokhzadian, J., Khajouei, R., & Ahmadian, L. (2015). Information seeking and retrieval skills of nurses: Nurses readiness for evidence based practice in hospitals of a medical university in Iran. *International journal of medical informatics, 84*(8), 570–577. https://doi.org/10.1016/j.ijmedinf.2015.03.008.

Flood, L. S., Gasiewicz, N., & Delpier, T. (2010). Integrating information literacy across a BSN curriculum. *Journal of Nursing Education, 49*(2), 101–104.

Forsman, H., Rudman, A., Gustavsson, P., Ehrenberg, A., & Wallin, L. (2010). Use of research by nurses during their first two years after graduating. *Journal of Advanced Nursing, 66*(4), 878–890. https://doi.org/10.1111/j.1365-2648.2009.05223.x.

Forster, M. (2013). A phenomenographic investigation into information literacy in nursing practice—Preliminary findings and methodological issues. *Nurse Education Today, 33*(10), 1237–1241. https://doi.org/10.1016/j.nedt.2012.05.027.

Franzen, S., & Bannon, C. M. (2016). Merging information literacy and evidence-based practice in an undergraduate health sciences curriculum map. *Communications in Information Literacy, 10*(2). https://doi.org/10.1007/s12630-009-9063-4.

Gardner, J. K., Kanaskie, M. L., Knehans, A. C., Salisbury, S., Doheny, K. K., & Schirm, V. (2016). Clinical method: Implementing and sustaining evidence-based practice through a nursing journal club. *Applied Nursing Research, 31,* 139–145. https://doi.org/10.1016/j.apnr.2016.02.001.

Garland Baird, L. M., & Miller, T. (2015). Factors influencing evidence-based practice for community nurses. *British Journal of Community Nursing, 20*(5), 233–242. https://doi.org/10.12968/bjcn.2015.20.5.233.

Gawlinski, A., & Rutledge, D. (2008). Selecting a model for evidence-based practice changes: A practical approach. *AACN Advanced Critical Care, 19*(3), 291–300.

Gerrish, K., & Cooke, J. (2013). Factors influencing evidence-based practice among community nurses. *Journal of Community Nursing, 27*(4), 98–101.

Goode, C. J., Fink, R. M., Krugman, M., Oman, K. S., & Traditi, L. K. (2011). The Colorado patient-centered interprofessional evidence-based practice model: A framework for transformation. *Worldviews on Evidence-Based Nursing, 8*(2), 96–105. https://doi.org/10.1111/j.1741-6787.2010.00208.x.

Hain, D. J., & Kear, T. M. (2015). Using evidence-based practice to move beyond doing things the way we have always done them. *Nephrology Nursing Journal, 42*(1), 11–21.

Hosking, J., Knox, K., Forman, J., Montgomery, L. A., Valde, J. G., & Cullen, L. (2016). Evidence into practice: Leading new graduate nurses to evidence-based practice through a nurse residency program. *Journal of PeriAnesthesia Nursing, 31*(3), 260–265. https://doi.org/10.1016/j.jopan.2016.02.006.

Ivanitskaya, L., O'Boyle, I., & Casey, A. M. (2006). Health information literacy and competencies of information age students: Results from the interactive online research readiness self-assessment (RRSA). *Journal of Medical Internet Research, 8*(2), e6.

Jackson, N. (2016). Incorporating evidence-based practice learning into a nurse residency program. *Journal of Nursing Administration, 46*(5), 278–283. https://doi.org/10.1097/NNA.0000000000000343.

Jacobs S. K., Rosenfeld P., Haber J. 2003 Information literacy as the foundation for evidence-based practice in graduate nursing education: A curriculum-integrated approach *Journal of Professional Nursing 19* 5: 320–328.

Kim, S. C., Ecoff, L., Brown, C. E., Gallo, A. M., Stichler, J. F., & Davidson, J. E. (2017). Benefits of a regional evidence-based practice fellowship program: A test of the ARCC model. *Worldviews on Evidence-Based Nursing, 14*(2), 90–98. https://doi.org/10.1111/wvn.12199.

Linton, M. J., & Prasun, M. A. (2013). Evidence-based practice: Collaboration between education and nursing management. *Journal of Nursing Management, 21*(1), 5–16. https://doi.org/10.1111/j.1365-2834.2012.01440.x.

Mackey, A., & Bassendowski, S. (2017). The history of evidence-based practice in nursing education and practice. *Journal of Professional Nursing, 33*(1), 51–55. https://doi.org/10.1016/j.profnurs.2016.06.009.

Mallion, J., & Brooke, J. (2016). Community- and hospital-based nurses' implementation of evidence-based practice: Are there any differences? *British Journal of Community Nursing, 21*(3), 148–154. https://doi.org/10.12968/bjcn.2016.21.3.148.

McCulley, C., & Jones, M. (2013). Fostering RN-to-BSN students' confidence in searching online for scholarly information on evidence-based practice. *Journal of Continuing Education in Nursing, 45*(1), 22–27.

McKeever, S., Twomey, B., Hawley, M., Lima, S., Kinney, S., & Newall, F. (2016). Engaging a nursing workforce in evidence-based practice: Introduction of a nursing clinical effectiveness committee. *Worldviews on Evidence-Based Nursing, 13*(1), 85–88. https://doi.org/10.1111/wvn.12119.

Melnyk, B. M. (2016). Culture eats strategy every time: What works in building and sustaining an evidence-based practice culture in healthcare systems. *Worldviews on Evidence-Based Nursing, 13*(2), 99–101. https://doi.org/10.1111/wvn.12161.

Melnyk, B., FineHolt-Overholt, E., Stillwell, S., & Williamson, K. (2010). The seven steps of evidence-based practice. *American Journal of Nursing, 110*(1), 51–53.

Meredith, E. K., Cohen, E., & Raia, L. V. (2010). Transformational leadership: Application of magnet's new empiric outcomes. *Nursing Clinics of North America, 45*(1), 49–64. https://doi.org/10.1016/j.cnur.2009.10.007.

Middlebrooks, R., Jr., Carter-Templeton, H., & Mund, A. R. (2016). Effect of evidence-based practice programs on individual barriers of workforce nurses: An integrative review. *Journal of Continuing Education in Nursing, 47*(9), 398–406. https://doi.org/10.3928/00220124-20160817-06.

Molteni, V. E., & Chan, E. K. (2015). Student confidence/overconfidence in the research process. *The Journal of Academic Librarianship, 41*(1), 2–8. https://doi.org/10.1016/j.acalib.2014.11.012.

Renolen, Å., & Hjälmhult, E. (2015). Nurses experience of using scientific knowledge in clinical practice: A grounded theory study. *Scandinavian Journal of Caring Sciences, 29*(4), 633–641. https://doi.org/10.1111/scs.12191.

Ryan, E. J. (2016). Undergraduate nursing students' attitudes and use of research and evidence-based practice–an integrative literature review. *Journal of clinical nursing, 25*(11–12), 1548–1556. https://doi.org/10.1111/jocn.13229.

Shaffer, S. T., Zarnowsky, C. D., Green, R. C., Chen Lim, M.-L., Holtzer, B. M., & Ely, E. A. (2013). Strategies from bedside nurse perspectives in conducting evidence-based practice projects to improve care. *Nursing Clinics of North America, 48*, 353–361. https://doi.org/10.1016/j.cnur.2013.01.004.

Solomons, N. M., & Spross, J. A. (2011). Evidence-based practice barriers and facilitators from a continuous quality improvement perspective: An integrative review. *Journal of Nursing Management, 19*(1), 109–120. https://doi.org/10.1111/j.1365-2834.2010.01144.x.

Stillwell, S. B. (2010). National survey shows the majority of nurses use very little research in the first 2 years after their graduation, highlighting a gap between research and clinical practice. *Evidence Based Nursing, 13*(4), 104. https://doi.org/10.1136/ebn.13.4.104.

Stombaugh, A., Sperstad, R., VanWormer, A., Jennings, E., Kishel, H., & Vogh, B. (2013). Using lesson study to integrate information literacy throughout the curriculum. *Nurse educator, 38*(4), 173–177. https://doi.org/10.1097/NNE.0b013e318296db56.

Swanberg, S.M., Dennison, C.C, Farrell, A., Machel, V., Marton, C., O'Brien, K.K., … Holyoke, A.N. 2016. Instructional methods used by health sciences librarians to teach evidence-based practice (EBP): A systematic review. Journal of the Medical Library Association10(3) 197–208. doi: https://doi.org/10.3163/1536-5050.104.3.004.

Tanner, A., Pierce, S., & Pravikoff, D. (2004). Readiness for evidence-based practice: Information literacy needs of nurses in the United States. *Studies in Health Technology and Informatics, 107*(Pt 2), 936–940.

Thomas, W. S. (2017). Nurse research rounds: In the spirit of inquiry. *Medical Reference Services Quarterly, 36*(2), 179–186. https://doi.org/10.1080/02763869.2017.1293988.

Thompson, C., Aitken, L., Doran, D., & Dowding, D. (2013). An agenda for clinical decision making and judgement in nursing research and education. *International Journal of Nursing Studies, 50*(12), 1720–1726. https://doi.org/10.1016/j.ijnurstu.2013.05.003.

Voldbjerg, S. L. (2016). Newly graduated nurses' use of knowledge sources: A meta-ethnography. *Journal of Advanced Nursing, 72*(8), 1751–1765. https://doi.org/10.1111/jan.12914.

Voldbjerg, S., Grønkjær, M., Wiechula, R., & Sørensen, E. (2017). Newly graduated nurses' use of knowledge sources in clinical decision-making: An ethnographic study. *Journal of Clinical Nursing, 26*(9–10), 1313–1327. https://doi.org/10.1111/jan.12914.

Waters, D., Crisp, J., Rychetnik, L., & Barratt, A. (2009). The Australian experience of nurses' preparedness of evidence-based practice. *Journal of Nursing Management, 17*, 510–518. https://doi.org/10.1111/j.1365-2834.2009.00997.x.

Wilson, M., Sleutel, M., Newcomb, P., Behan, D., Walsh, J., Wells, J., & Baldwin, K. (2015). Empowering nurses with evidence-based practice environments: Surveying magnet®, pathway to excellence®, and non-magnet facilities in one healthcare system. *Worldviews on Evidence-Based Nursing, 12*(1), 12–21. https://doi.org/10.1111/wvn.12077.

Yoder, L. H., Kirkley, D., McFall, D. C., Kirksey, K. M., StalBaum, A. L., & Sellers, D. (2014). Staff nurses' use of research to facilitate evidence-based practice. *Journal of Nursing*, *114*(9), 26–38. https://doi.org/10.1097/01.NAJ.0000453752.93269.43.

FURTHER READING

Baker, A. (2001). Crossing the quality chasm: A new health system for the 21st century. *BMJ: British Medical Journal, 323*(7322), 1192.

Ivanitskaya, L. V., Hanisko, K. A., Garrison, J. A., Janson, S. J., & Vibbert, D. (2012). Developing health information literacy: A needs analysis from the perspective of preprofessional health students. *Journal of the Medical Library Association, 100*(4), 227–283. https://doi.org/10.3163/1536-5050.100.4.009.

INDEX

Note: Page numbers followed by *f* indicate figures and *t* indicate tables.

Printed in the United States
By Bookmasters